George Francis Train

Speech on Irish independence and English neutrality

Delivered before the Fenian Congress and Fenian chiefs at the

Philadelphia Academy of Music

George Francis Train

Speech on Irish independence and English neutrality
Delivered before the Fenian Congress and Fenian chiefs at the Philadelphia Academy of Music

ISBN/EAN: 9783337124236

Printed in Europe, USA, Canada, Australia, Japan

Cover: Foto ©Thomas Meinert / pixelio.de

More available books at **www.hansebooks.com**

TRAIN ON IRISH INDEPENDENCE.

SPEECH OF

GEORGE FRANCIS TRAIN,

ON

IRISH INDEPENDENCE,

AND

ENGLISH NEUTRALITY.

DELIVERED BEFORE THE

"FENIAN CONGRESS" & "FENIAN CHIEFS,"

AT THE

PHILADELPHIA ACADEMY OF MUSIC, OCTOBER 18th, 1865,
IN THE PRESENCE OF SIX THOUSAND PERSONS.

Philadelphia:
T. B. PETERSON & BROTHERS, 306 CHESTNUT STREET.

PRICE 25 CENTS.

SPEECH

OF

GEORGE FRANCIS TRAIN,

ON

IRISH INDEPENDENCE

AND

ENGLISH NEUTRALITY.

DELIVERED BEFORE THE

"FENIAN CONGRESS" AND "FENIAN CHIEFS,"

AT THE

PHILADELPHIA ACADEMY OF MUSIC, OCTOBER 18, 1865,

IN THE PRESENCE OF SIX THOUSAND PERSONS.

Philadelphia:

T. B. PETERSON & BROTHERS,

306 CHESTNUT STREET.

SPEECH

OF

GEORGE FRANCIS TRAIN,

BEFORE THE

FENIAN CONGRESS AND FENIAN CHIEFS,

DELIVERED AT THE

ACADEMY OF MUSIC, PHILADELPHIA,

ON

Wednesday Evening, October 18th, 1865,

IN THE PRESENCE OF SIX THOUSAND PERSONS.

Notwithstanding the terrible inclemency of the night—the rain pouring down in torrents—the Fenian delegates in session at Philadelphia are moving to and fro on their important mission. You meet them everywhere, but they are so reticent, so guarded in their conversation it is almost impossible to know anything of their doings. The whole matter is rapt in an impenetrable mystery, but the earnestness of the men—their dignified manners—the fact that they represent all parts of the country; that generals, editors, bankers, lawyers and merchants are among them; that they pay their own expenses, represent 300,000 organized men, all tends to give importance to their action. They shrink from publicity, ignore popular applause, and count no outside assistance.

For the first time, the convention were moved into a spontaneous outburst of enthusiasm. The President of the Central Council appeared about seven o'clock and read the Secretary of State's telegraphic dispatch to George Francis Train denouncing the calumny of the English press. The convention rose to their feet and made the welkin ring in cheers for Mr. Seward, the President, for Mr. Train and Ireland. The convention then at once adjourned and proceeded to the Academy of Music, to hear Mr. Train, and headed by their band playing a national air, they marched six hundred strong, tramp, tramp, tramp, through the rain, with their Irish guards, dressed in the picturesque garb of the Irish army, carrying banners and the American flag. The stage of the Academy of Music was crowded with Fenian chiefs. All the Head Centres were there, but many had to leave the stage and take their chances with the crowded audience.

The distinguished lecturer was introduced by Lieutenant-Colonel Roberts, of New York, President of the Central Council, in the following words:—

LADIES AND GENTLEMEN:—I have the honor to introduce to you this evening the distinguished lecturer, who speaks as a free, enlightened American citizen, in behalf of Irish Republicanism. (Applause.) He is the embodiment, I trust in Heaven, of the sentiment that animates the heart of every true American, for liberty in every quarter of the globe. Allow me to introduce to you George Francis Train.

The deafening and long-continued cheering with which the orator of the evening was received having somewhat subsided, he came forwarded in open dress—lavender kids, white vest, dress coat, and brass buttons—hat in his hand, and stated he should take as his text the last slanders of the London press.

MR. TRAIN'S SPEECH.

AMERICANS! For Irishmen are as much Americans as those who came to Jamestown or to Plymouth ten genera-tions ago. [Loud cheers.] I would that I could pass those cheers "along the line," and over the ocean to the men of Ireland, who at this moment stand upon tiptoe to catch the reverberations of just such cheers from this side of the water. (Applause.)

> They say that dear old Ireland has foes on every side,
> Who envy her, her conquests, her race, her fame, her pride,
> The Sassenach exulting vaunts all her strength is past,
> Dreaming her intruding sons shall bite the dust at last.
> > But let them say whate'er they will,
> > Her banner bears no stain;
> > The deeds old Ireland once has done,
> > She yet can do again. .
> > > [*Tremendous excitement and applause.*]

(Mr. Train then read extracts from Mr. Seward's speech in the Senate on General Shield's motives in 1851, about petition-ing England for the release of Smith O'Brien and John Mit-chell, and applied Mr. Seward's remarks to Ireland at the present time. . The speech was received with great excitement and applause. We wish we had space to give it entire. Mr. Train then rung the charges in the *Time's* last leader, calling the Irish fools, tailors, ninnies.) Those are the words they have called the northern armies these four years. That reminds me of a little story that our friend here General Sweeney, the one-armed Fenian hero—told me an hour ago. (Cheers.) During the American Revolution the London press used the same slang terms. The theatre was the place for satire. The popular play was one ridiculing the American army as composed of vulgar tradesmen. One scene was something like this: British officer—What is your name? John Smith. What is your business? Tailor. (Here is where the laugh comes in.) Your name, sir? Tom Jones. Business? Printer. (Sneering laugh.) Yours? Cobbler. (Loud laughter from the British audience.) Just at this moment some one shouted, with a peculiar nasal voice, Hurrah! Hurrah! Hurrah! The audience were startled. The voice, louder than before, yelled out. That is the best thing yet. The entire British army whipped by a lot of tailors, cobblers and printers. (Loud laughter and cheers.)

"A batch (says the telegraph) of demented printers." Three cheers for the Irish press that can so startle a thousand-year-old monarchy into hysterics. (Loud laughter.) "A pugnacious tailor and mad hatter, a score of shopboys as mad as the hatter, a few publicans and a distracted militiaman." Hurrah for the tailor pugnacious that can shake an empire out of its nightmare. Andrew Johnson forever. (Loud cheers.) Hurrah for the Irish militiaman that braves the trained cohorts of England! Hurrah for the Irish shopboys that can make the old lady jump out of her bed in her night cap and night robe to order the British army to arrest them! (Laughter and cheers.) Hurrah for the mad hatter who valorously dares England to tear up Magna Charta, throw the British Constitution into the Thames, and outrage all the sacred rights of which Englishmen are so proud. What a terrible crime (said the *Times* a little while ago) it is to make military arrests, open mail bags and suppress newspapers. Ah, Delane, we have you now on the gridiron. (Loud laughter.) Sir John Falstaff, thank God! was not born in Ireland. (Cheers and laughter.)

> A wail from haunted battle-field ascends!
> As from their caverns hermit winds complain,
> And history shudders, as she o'er them bends,
> To hear : "In vain! In vain!"

Had I been dwarfed down in this rebellion to a pot-house politician, a Chicago wigwam demagogue, a Baltimore Convention shoddy contractor, a Cleveland caucus bunkumite, (laughter), a political Major-General, or even a Senator from Massachusetts, (loud laughter and cheers), what I say to-night would have little effect; but, inasmuch as I have preserved my individuality while a hetacomb of ambitious men are piled up along the roadside, and inasmuch as I have played the patriot without demanding pay for the patriotism [cheers] —defended the nation's integrity and honor without boring for office or Government patronage—inasmuch as I have stood by the rights of the white men, and for twenty years on all occasions and everywhere defended Ireland and the Irish (loud cheers, the audience rising and waving their hats for several minutes)—I have certainly strong opinions on the events of the age, that I will oblige mankind to respect. (Applause, and bully for Train.)

I ask no favors of the public. I have no faith in popular applause. I feel with Henry Clay, I would rather be right than be President. (That's it.) My platform is easily comprehended. France for the French, Italy for the Italians, Germany for the Germans, Asia, for the Asiatics, Africa for the Africans, (laughter), America, for the Americans, (applause), and Ireland for the Irish, is God's law. But Hungary, Poland, Venice and Ireland, show that "man's inhumanity to man makes countless thousands mourn."

> The Green Flag of old Ireland,
>   Yes, yet thy folds shall shine
> Across the land which gave thee birth,
>   As Freedom's blessed sign!
> What Irish heart would pour not
>   His life-blood in the dust,
> To keep thee there for evermore
>   In tenderness and trust?

In this connection, as pertinent to the remarks I am about to make, allow me to read an extract or two from late Eng-

lish newspapers, and I will make that the text of whatever in
a conversational way I may say to you this evening. I quote
from the speech of Digby Seymour, which you may all have
seen in the papers received by the last mail. A most insulting
speech by a bankrupt English barrister:—"Why, what is a
Fenian? A discontented Irishman in search of a grievance—
*a tool for American insolence to menace the peace of Europe with
—a thing in the lash, with which Yankee buncombe threatens to
whip creation.* (Cheers and laughter.) Was Phillips a Fenian? No.

Allow me to quote from another authority to set the matter
right. Speaking of the English ministry and the wrongs of
Ireland, my authority says: "Misfortune teaches them no
mercy, or experience wisdom. Vindictive in prosperity, servile in defeat, timid in the field, vacillating in the cabinet,
suspicious among themselves, discontent among their followers, piety active in subservience to their sycophantic
clergy, power passive but in subjugating the people, they
blunder on from one expedient to the other, refusing to let
go their hold on the throat of Ireland." Do you recognize
the language? It was addressed by that great Irish orator
Phillips, to the corrupt ministry of England. (Long continued
applause.)

But to return to the speech of Digby Seymour, whose argu-
ment I take as that of the British government, in whose behalf it was made. He says that Phillips was always loyal to
the throne and institutions of his country:—"Was Curran a
Fenian? No; the warmth of patriotism never consumed the
adamant of his loyalty." Now I will read from Curran in
exposition of his sentiments:—"How have the last few years
been employed by the English, but in destroying the land-
marks of rights and duties and obligations; in substituting
sounds in the place of sense; in substituting a vile and cant-
ing Methodism in the place of social duty and practical honor;
in suffering virtue to degenerate into pleasure, and morality
into hypocrisy and affectation."

Do you recognize the language? They are the stirring words of Curran to the corrupt politicians of his day. Digby Seymour is greatly mistaken in his authority. He then speaks of O'Connell: "Was O'Connell a Fenian? No. When he spoke from the hall of Tara to ten thousand of his people, he never uttered a disloyal thought against the British throne or Constitution." If he did not, it was time he did. (Great cheering.)

I now quote from the *Saturday Review*, of London: "Besides these men and the tailor commanding, there are bricklayers and watermen, clerks and printers in abundance, with of course, one journalist to do the felony in the *Irish People*, which is a feeble reproduction of the once famous *Nation*. A stray militiaman or two may be noticed in the lists, but none of the trans-atlantic branch of the society, which was supposed to have attained the most formidable dimensions; and in the whole catalogue there is not one man of education and position to play over again the mock-heroic part to which poor, silly Smith O'Brien was prompted by his inordinate vanity."

I now quote from the *London Times*: "The priests denounce them with the vigorous and telling rhetoric of their order; the farmers will have nothing to do with them; newspapers which might have been counted upon to defend Ireland against the Saxon, exhaust the vocabulary of contempt against the too eager revolutionists. They are fools, ninnies, mere tailors and shop-boys playing at treason."

Now, really, gentlemen, is it possible that fools, ninnies, and shop-boys, can so frighten the great English nation, that the whole British army should be called out, and the British navy sent up the shores of Ireland? (Laughter.) Mind you, these are the stock terms that England always uses. American soldiers who are here to-night, they called you the same names during our late civil war. They called you fools and ninnies. And when they sneered at a tailor, they did it— the *London Times* did it—well knowing the people of the United States had elected a tailor to be the head of this great nation. And you may tell Andrew Johnson that this insult was not intended for the Irish, but for him, because of his being the chief of a free people.

Their impudence in pretending to represent Ireland is unbearable; and anything they may get at the next Assizes will be richly deserved. But this is not all. Even the land which is the birth-place of Fenianism repudiates them. Not only is the American Government suspected of being guilty of friendly intentions towards England, but leading men in the States and important organs of opinion declare Fenianism to be an imposture on their side of the ocean," etc.

I have other extracts here stating that Mr. Seward and other members of our Government had informed the British Secret Office of the Fenian movement. Now I know that must be false, and for this reason. I remember (and I am indebted to Mr. Gallien, of St. Louis, for reminding me of it) that in 1851, when Shields came in with his resolution about Smith O'Brien, Mr. Seward made a speech in reply to the Irish delegation, and in that speech gave expression to these sentiments:—

"The policy of England was the error of the age, and the fault of her systems. This is her sufficient apology; but on an occasion like this, Ireland is entitled to a dispassionate vindication, and is entitled to our respect and our sympathy. That sympathy derives intenseness from the conceded virtues and proverbial virtues of Irish people. The plains of Waterloo, and heights of Quebec bear witness that they are brave and skilful in war—like the Greeks, they have in their decline enchanted the world with wit, and song, and eloquence. Confiding and generous to a fault, while in their whole history does not occur one instance of the indulgence of unlawful ambition. Is not, then, the tribute proposed by this resolution due from the United States, on such an occasion, to such a people? I shall be answered—that question of clemency is not for us but for Great Britain. This is true; but men and nations are swayed by perseverance. It may be said, that while as individuals we may lawfully sympathize, we cannot express these sympathies as a nation. This seems to me equivalent to saying, that we may indulge in unavailing sentiment, but shall not exercise active benevolence. There is only one code of morality for mankind, in all circumstances, conditions, and relations, and in direct and comprehensive obligations, bind them equally as subjects, citizens, and individuals, and sects; but it is said that we may not lawfully intervene in the affairs of another sovereign State."—This is the point. What does Mr. Seward say on the subject?—"So, indeed, we may not, for judicious purposes, or even beneficent ones by force, but under law of nations, as perfected on Christian principles. The several civilized States are regarded as constituting one great commonwealth, while no one can rightfully encroach on absolute right of another, or interfere with the conduct of its domestic affairs."

He goes on to discuss that question, but I will pass on to another paragraph:—"The people of Ireland are affiliated to us by consanguinity, as we are to the people of Great Britain. Surely the younger may, without offense, offer its mediation upon a point of difference between the elder branches of a common family. And what if Great Britain should take offense? We no longer stand in awe of her power, and she knows that right well. If she should repulse a benevolent and lawful suggestion, why then she would be in the wrong, and we should be justified. But Great Britain will not take offense," etc. He makes one more point. "Sir, while it is thus certain that we may with confidence appeal to Great Britain, the claim of Ireland upon us for intervention is unanswerable."

If this were so then, I would like to know how it is to-day, when Irish blood has flowed like water upon every battle-field where Irishmen could fight for the Union, the Constitution, and the Government.

"But for our instruction and example during a period of near seventy years, Smith O'Brien and his associates, would

never have attempted to lift up from degradation his father-
land. We have maintained nearly all that Ireland has lost
by her exhaustion. Her poverty has added to our wealth;
her growing weakness to our own increasing strength. Could
Ireland have retained or have taken back, in the hour of
need, the political forces which she has given up to us, that
attempted revolution would have been successful." (Applause.)

I merely ask Mr. Seward to remember what he said in
1851. But knowing that the reports to which I have referred
were false, I yesterday telegraphed to Mr. Seward at Auburn,
at which place he speaks to-night; and where he is now pro-
bably reiterating what he here says to me. In answer to
my despatch I received this telegram. I will read both
despatches;—

EVERETT HOUSE, *New York, October* 15, 1865.

To the Hon. WILLIAM H. SEWARD, *Auburn, New York.*

I address the Fenian Brotherhood Wednesday night, Philadelphia, Academy; Irish Congress present. May I deny
English assertion that Irish arrests are made through your
advices?

The following is Mr. Seward's reply, which was made
within half an hour after he received my message:—

AUBURN, *N. Y,, October* 16, 1865.

To GEORGE F. TRAIN, Everett House, New York:—

I cannot depart from my habit of leaving my vindication
against calumnies to an intelligent country, and a candid
world.

W. H. SEWARD.

· (The reading of the above reply created the wildest enthusiasm, rounds of cheers being repeatedly given by the audience for William H. Seward, Andrew Johnson, and George
Francis Train.)

Now, there is the lie direct to the *Morning Post*, to the London *Times*, to the *Saturday Review*, and to the London *Telegraph*. (Cheers.) You can have nothing more straightforward than that; and I knew it must be so or I would not have sent the dispatch. I believe that is the first official denial of these unfounded reports that reach us by every mail from across the water.

Now, it is about time for America to understand her position. I am sick and tired of hearing Americans talking of England as the mother-land. I thought it had been explained long ago that England was not our mother-land. (Applause.)

Three years ago I made a speech on this stage, and I remember having seen in the London press, in one day, eight editorials upon it. (Laughter.) I rather think that what I say now may reach them also. I want them to understand that England is not our mother-land, but that the first man who came to this country from Europe was Christopher Columbus. (Applause.) He was not an Englishman, but an Italian. The second was Americus Vespucci. He was not an Englishman, but a Portuguese. The third was Sebastian Cabot, a Spaniard. Then, who settled New York? The Dutch. Was England their mother-land? Who settled New Jersey? The Swedes. Was England their mother-land? Who settled Delaware? The Danes. Who settled Baltimore and Maryland? The Irish Catholics. Was England their mother-land? Who settled South Carolina? The Huguenots. Was England their mother-land? Who settled Florida? The Spanish. Louisiana? The French. I have looked at the record, and I tell you that to-day, from the Lakes to the Gulf, and from Ocean to Ocean, we have not ten per cent. of English blood in our veins. (Great applause.) We have Irish blood in far greater proportion, the same that has flowed forth like water upon every battle-field of the war in behalf of our country. (Applause.)

You know that the wisdom of Solomon was never better illustrated than in the case of the false mother, when, in order to determine the true parent, he ordered the child to be cut in twain. We have found during this war who were our friends and who were our enemies. England is not our mother-land; England is our grandmother-land. (Laughter.) It is about time, as I told them in the halls of London, that America should have a mother-land of her own. It occurs to me that the place in which a man is born is his mother-land. I happened to be born in Massachusetts, and I apologize to the audience for it. (Laughter.) Seven generations were born under the same roof, and therefore I can say England is not my mother-land.

And allow me to say here, that if it should be said that I am endeavoring to ally myself with every or any popular sentiment that may arise, I would merely ask a reference to the facts. I am usually against the tide. Anything can go out with the stream—straws, lemon-peelings, stinking fish—it is only a strong fish that goes against the tide. Just as in the case of mankind generally; there are negative and positive men in the world. The negative man goes down the stream quietly, and with no effort on his part; the positive man goes up against the stream, gaining steadily, it may be only an inch or two at a time; but the people on the beach are watching him.

I stood alone in England for two years fighting for Ireland, for America, and for the common rights of humanity. (Great applause.) I told the committee who invited me here that I was not a Fenian, but that I had been an Irishman, and a better one than many of those whom you have elevated to high positions, and who, when thus elevated, have turned from you. I tell you, Irishmen, you are sneered at; but you are fools to be sneered at any longer. I say, that one-seventeenth of this entire population is Celtic; that you, Irishmen, are American citizens, and it is your own fault, if, instead of sending to Congress, miserable politicians, who will sell you out, you do not send there next fall, one hundred Irishmen.

But to return to my text. I propose to commend to English lips the same poisoned chalice which English cun-

ning had prepared for our own country. Lord John Russell
said (I am merely changing the word, not the sense) that
Ireland fought for Independence, England for Empire; and,
during the late war, England applied the same declaration to
our own case in favor of the South. All that I ask now is,
that America shall acknowledge Ireland as a belligerent.
(Great cheering.)

> The Green Flag of Old Ireland !
>   A blessing on each fold,
> More tender than the earth's green breast,
>   More bright than burnished gold !
> What Irish bosom thrills not
>   With patriotic dreams,
>   While here, in free America,
>   Thine Emerald beauty streams !

Our Government cannot very well interfere, for we know
now the law of nations. England has taught us what to do
in such a case. (Laughter.) What our Government must do
is to remain strictly neutral (applause), while our Lairds, our
Lyndseys, and our Gregorys, fit out a hundred, and, if necessary, a thousand *Alabamas*, *Sumters*, and *Shenandoahs*, to
sweep British commerce from the face of the earth. (Applause.)
We must remain *strictly neutral*. We must put on board these
pirate ships any quantity of Enfield rifles, Colt's revolvers,
and munitions of war, with a view to running the blockade of
Belfast, of Dublin, or of Cork. (Great applause.) And if the
pickets already on the advance—"the fools and ninnies"—
can create such dismay as they have created in the great
English nation, what will be the condition of things when
O'Mahony moves with the entire army ! (Cheers.)

> Ye sons of liberty, awake ! your hearths and altars are at stake;
> Arise, arise, for Ireland's sake, and strike for John O'Mahony,
> Your Irish Eagle is not dead ; again his giant wings are spread,
> To sweep upon old England's head, and on with John O'Mahony.
> What soul but scorns the coward slave ? But liberty if for the brave.
> Our cry be Ireland or the grave, and on with John O'Mahony.

(Great cheering, renewed again and again.)

In the discussion halls of London I told Englishmen to remember, when they sneered at Ireland, that they had no soldiers of their own at all. And your great barristers—your Grattans and Phillipses and O'Donnells and O'Connells—all these men, I told them, had come from Ireland, and that their great chieftains all over the world were Irishmen. I told them that the great man in Spain to-day (Marshal O'Donnell, the Premier) was an Irishman; that the great man who won the battle of Kinchello, MacNear, the Duke of Magenta, was an Irishman; that the leading man in the Austrian army to-day, Field-Marshal Nugent, was an Irishman. I told them they had produced only one great victory, and that was achieved under an Irishman, the Duke of Wellington. [Was he a renegade Irishman? Yes.] The Irish do not live alone in Ireland; they are dispered from their homes. There are two millions in England, five millions of Irish in America, and five hundred thousand in Australia. Under many an English coat you will find an Irish heart. For the poor laws under English rule brought on the famine, and starved or drove them from their homes. Then America showed she was Irish in heart by sending out ship loads of food.

When Englishmen asked why we did not put down the war, he told them we were fighting Americans, not Englishmen. He had been complimented about speaking good English. In future we should speak the American language. In Russia the laws prescribe that the American language shall be taught. This country taught the English how to speak.

I told them that the leading men in Australia were Irishmen; and you will find Murphy, and O'Shaughnessy, and Duffy there to-day. I showed them that the famine in Ireland was produced by the poor laws and cruel treatment of that unfortunate country by England, and that America showed herself to be Irish in sending out ships of bread for suffering Irishmen and their starving families. When they asked me, "Why don't you put down the war in your own country?" I replied that it was simply because we were fighting Americans; that, had we been fighting Englishmen, we would readily have done it. (Applause.)

When they complimented me on my using such good English, I gave them to understand that, in my opinion at least, the King's English in their hands was certainly not more improved than in mine, and that our nation might ere long adopt a distinctive language for its own use. A special ukase has been passed in Russia requiring the language of that empire to be taught in all the colonies within the jurisdiction of the Czar; and, therefore, why should we not follow the example thus set for our imitation?

I told them in England that we had given them a grammar by Lindley Murray, a dictionary and many other elementary works on the language, and that they could not spell the commonest words. I asked them to spell "soldier," and they commenced with a *less* and a *ho* and went on with a *hell* and a *de* and a *hi* and a *he* and a *har.*

(The lecturer, at this point, digressed from his subject to notice the affected manners of certain classes in English society. His peculiar representations were very amusing, and we regret our inability to reproduce them.)

Why, my friends, you know there are forty different dialects in as many counties in England. You go down into Wales; and there to pronounce the smallest word you are obliged to open your mouth so very wide, that the back of your head resembles an island. Yet they talk of their ability to speak English! Why they know nothing about it, and much less about our country. They think that that little movement in Ireland is the Fenian movement. Why that is but a rocket, a blue light; nothing is done yet. There is an enormous power in secresy. No one knows your secret movements. No one knows what the Fenians are doing. There is a great power in keeping behind the scenes.

Allow me to say one word in regard to our debt. The

2

English have said, "Why, you are rolling up an immense national debt." I say that that is so, and I ask them what right have they to monopolize all the debt of the world. Said I to them, "We will have a national debt one of these days that will make you ashamed of yourselves." But it requires only a retrospective glance at the debt of England to establish in your minds the fact that she is the mere pasturage of the aristocracy. It is terrible to see how they have fooled the people. England has sent her George Thompsons all over this country in order to emancipate our slaves. Then it is our duty, as England has done so much for our blacks, to do something for her whites.

Mind you, the idea has been that when Exeter Hall took snuff we should sneeze, and when the *London Times* has laid an egg we should cackle. What I propose now is that, as England has emancipated four millions of our black slaves, we should send out a few George Thompsons to lecture all over England, with a view to the emancipation of her white slaves. There are six millions of able-bodied Englishmen who are not even on a par with the negro slaves in the Southern section of our country; for while our forefathers admitted that a negro was three-fifths of a man, and thus far provided that he should be represented, the poor white people of England have no votes. England degrades them even below the level of our lately enslaved negroes.

Who gets the thirty millions that are annually taken from the Exchequer of England for the expenses of the army? The people? No; it rests simply with the lords and titled nobility. The people have nothing to do with it. You will find that England is pastured off among thirty thousand families. The whole country is in the hands of thirty thousand families, and the entire national debt of England is in the hands of three hundred thousand families. I sincerely believe that as soon as the movement takes place in Ireland, which has not yet commenced, the national debt of England will fall like that [stamping his foot]. (Applause.)

They have upheld it by the most gigantic paper-money system that the world has ever seen; and America for the last twenty years has been giving her the means wherewith to pay her national debt. Now let me tell you where the trouble is. England has ruined all the nations of the world —all that she could ruin being those who took her counsel. Look at the sterile lands and deserted ports and empty warehouses of Portugal. England ruined Portugal by her miserable free-trade policy. Again, go to Turkey. Turkey has been destroyed by England forcing her policy down the throats of that people.

You should always bear in mind that England's track around the world is one track of blood. It is simply the strong against the weak. Go where you will her record is the same in the case of every nation she has had in her power. Wherever England has coveted the division of a nation, she has introduced among the people of that nation some bone of contention. In Ireland, it has been religion—the Catholic against the Protestant. In this country, the negro was to break us up; and now she has sent here her emissaries to divide the Fenian Brotherhood by fomenting a Catholic and Protestant war. Augustus Cæsar prolonged a little while a misspent life in a singular and most odious state: but the Roman Emperor only ruined virgins; it was England that destroyed nations.

I think it is time that the people of America should throw aside the miserable toadyism of the last hundred years, and be a nation of themselves, for we are now twenty-one years of age. (Applause.) We have been treated badly by England. You remember to have read of that little shivering band who came over here that they might have freedom of speech. The points of their career may be briefly summed. They cut down the tree and then built a school-house. The little colony grew. England taxed them. They paid the taxes. Time passed on. More trees down—more school-houses—a church. Then England taxed them more. They paid the taxes. But England wanting more money to carry on the war against France, imposed more taxes. They refused, and asked for representation in the British Parliament. You remember the rest. Out came the order—"We demand." Then came the stamp act, then the port bill. Overboard went the tea and up went the flag. (Great applause.)

The Declaration of a nation's independence was read from Independence Hall down here, by an Irishman. It was received right from the hands of Jefferson by an Irishman, and was first copied by an Irish editor. (Great applause.) Let me hear no more about the Irish being here by sufferance. They watched over the cradle of the country. They have been with it in its youth, and stood by it in its manhood. You will find that the very Capitol in which we hold our Congress, was presented to Washington by a Carroll, a splendid specimen of a noble Irishman. (Applause.)

All through our early history, it will be found that the Irish were conspicuous. It was a newly arrived major-general that crossed the border, and marched on Quebec, and fell there—Major-General Montgomery. Sullivan, at Bunker Hill, was an Irishman. Mad. Anthony Wayne, of Stony Point, was an Irishman. But thus in our infancy, and while we were yet a child in the cradle, we kicked England out of the house. Time passed on; our country increased in extent and population, and then England, in order to carry on a war with Bonaparte, took our sailors from our ships, you remember.

We told her that the flag covered the American citizen on the water as well as on the land. Again we fought, and again we kicked her about. Time passed on; and then she found she could not fight us with armies, for England is not a fighting nation—she has always fought with the hired soldiery, with Hessians in our Revolution, and with Swiss soldiers in the Crimea (and I had occasion to tell her people that so

many quarts of beer and so many pounds of mutton-chop
would fight). (Laughter and applause.) When she found
that she could not fight us openly, she sent her emissaries to
stir up feelings of sectional strife and bigotry, and finally
kindled the embers of political disaffection into a blaze of
civil war.

(At this point the speaker again alluded to the ignorance of
Englishmen concerning the current events of the day in this
country, and illustrated his meaning by personal anecdotes
which repeatedly brought down the house in rounds of
laughter and applause. The first illustration was that of a
cockney Englishman, who, after many hums and haws, in-
quired of the speaker, whether he was from Boston, and a
reply being given in the affirmative, expressed his desire to
know whether Boston was not one of the slave States. To
this the speaker replied, by good-naturedly assuring his in-
terrogator that Boston was noted for its abolition sentiments,
and that Mr. Dred Scott was mayor of that city. Another
inquisitive Englishman, desirous of stating the full particulars
concerning the Professor Webster murder case, which oc-
curred some years ago in Boston, informed Mr. Train that
he had just noticed by the last mail, that the Hon. Daniel
Webster, in a fit of aberration of mind, while in the prepara-
tion of his great dictionary, had murdered the Rev. Theodore
Parker. On another occasion, during the visit of Grantley
Berkeley to this country, while looking from the window of
the Fifth Avenue Hotel, New York, upon a fine sleighing
prospect (the season being winter), that gentleman expressed
to Mr. Train a desire to take a sleigh ride, who immediately
ordered John to put a couple of buffaloes in the steady and
take Mr. Berkeley out. "Oh, no!" interrupted the frightened
gentleman, "it does not make any difference to me, but I
would much prefer if you would use horses."

The lecturer then proceeded, referring to the higher classes
of England as follows :—

You know that in England, there is the army, the navy, and the church. They send the elder sons of the nobility to govern India, Australia, Nova Scotia, etc.; and the younger sons must be provided for, and are accordingly sent to college and educated all alike. Well, then it is a toss-up for which shall go in the army, which shall go in the navy, and which shall enter the church. Nine times out of ten, the one naturally fitted for the church goes to the army, while the military man goes to the church.

The consequences are, that they have got a rotten army and a rotten navy. The Bank of England is rotten to the core. I do not believe that to-day Rothschild can pay a shilling to the pound. And I sincerely believe, that two-thirds of those rotten old documents that have been handed down for three or four hundred years are forgeries, if we may judge, mind you, by what we have seen. (Applause.)

Look at Canada! No one can excite me more effectually than by saying that Americans want to annex Canada. An American coming from Canada to his own country, feels as if he had emerged from the darkness of night into the light of day. In America, we have labor-saving machines. We take a tree; staves cut, hoops on, and a barrel is made, and for three, four, or five cents it may be purchased. In Canada they cannot make it at all.

As a fair illustration of the two people, take the case of an American and a Canadian standing upon the bank of a canal. Says the Canadian to the American, "You can't jump across." "No, but I can throw you across." "I'll bet you can't," says the Canadian; "put up your money." The money is wagered; and the American takes the Canadian brother by the collar and the slack of his nether garments, and throws him half way across—splash into the water. He picks himself up, wades ashore and claims the money as having won the bet. "No, you've not won," says the American, "I missed the first time; but I'll throw you all day but I'll do it."

No, we want nothing to do with Canada. There are a great many Irishmen in Canada whom we stand by; but we do not want to annex that God-forsaken land. Have you ever seen an old water-logged ship coming into port from a foreign country? That is England. When she comes into port, notice the long sea-grass, the barnacles hanging to her sides—India, Nova Scotia, Canada, Van Diemen's Land—all hanging to the old rotten hull, and gradually bearing her down to the bottom.

What Canada should do, and had she any independence at all she would, would be to combine Prince Edward's Island, Newfoundland, Nova Scotia, and Canada into a confederation for an independent nation, under the idea of "Canada for the Canadians." I have been in Australia, and I sincerely believe that Van Diemen's Land, New Zealand, South Australia, and Victoria, will again hoist the "five stars" that I saw floating in 1852, during that little revolution that was gotten up there. (Applause.)

You, of course, understand that these remarks are *strictly neutral*. (Laughter.) England is now blackguarding us through the press, and I will tell you, Mr. Roberts, what you might do at this time. Go over and give $60,000 to Delaney, of the London *Times*. Then buy up Simpson, of the London *Post*, and Beresford Hope, of the *Saturday Review*.

The way to get hold of that people is to give them a few bonds, for as we have seen in the case of the distribution of the Confederate bonds, there can be no appeal to their hearts which will exert a greater influence than that which is made through the medium of their pockets. I repeat, wherever we turn in the history of nations, we find that England has committed some gigantic crime.

The Detroit Commercial Convention was a damaging disgrace to America—got up by Canadians, managed by Blue Noses, and steered by the English. The Hon. Joseph Howe, of Nova Scotia, pulled the wires. Does America know that

he was one of our bitterest opponents in this war ? I heard
him deliver an anti-American speech in the Forum Discussion Hall, London, where he grossly insulted John G. Winter,
of Columbus, Georgia, and when I rose to reply he bolted
from the room. I wish I had been at Detroit to reply to
him, you would only have found a grease spot on the floor.
(Laughter.) Mr. Seward made the only point in sending
Potter there to snub the Convention, and he did it well.
Canada has been howling ever since.

Mr. Train again ridiculed the idea of Americans wishing
Canada. Why, I would not recommend my Fenian friends
around me to think for a moment of establishing an Irish
republic there. God has blasted the energies of that people.
Ten years in Scheiferderher's Hydropathic Institute would
not wash the corruption, indolence and imbecility out of that
miserable country. (Loud laughter.) That illustrates the
stupidity of the Canadians. So long as they can draw
money out of England they will keep on sucking. • The
greatest swindle of any was the twenty million sterling
robbed from England in building the Grand Trunk Railway.
That was the last sugar-tit. (Laughter.) The capital is sunk,
the railroad wants repairing, the rails are worn out, the rolling
stock used up, and the receipts not enough to pay ordinary ·
expenses. The English party who are rolling over the land
and condescend to allow the American people to toady to
them, as we always do, are trying to galvanize the Grand
Trunk into life again, by bridging Niagara and connecting it
with the Atlantic and Great Western. Old Punch says:
Never chain a live man to a corpse. Those Englishmen
who are being banqueted everywhere, are all gentlemen, and
have been friends of ours, so I will not fire on them just yet,
on account of their having been invited and are the guests of
an Irish American, James McHenry, who was joint partner
with me in giving you Irish Pennsylvanians the Atlantic
and Great Western Railway.

No, we don't want and won't have Canada. France in-
tends recapturing Quebec. Napoleon bides his time. The
Fenian Brotherhood in Canada is organized in every town,
but the organization is different from the American.

England nurses her shiftless children by committing crimes
on other nationalities. A young law student reminded me
last night of the trial of Warren Hastings, the most stupen-
dous legal mockery ever imposed upon a people, the grandest
judicial farce ever enacted. (Applause.) The agent of the
British East India Company tried for that which he did at
their order. It was England arraigned at the bar, for the
East India Company was England. It was England against
whom the Irishmen, Burke and Sheridan, thundered, and
England was convicted and bearded with eternal infamy,
though the nominal offender escaped. ("That's so," and
"Shame on England.")

Her morning drum beat, to use a Websterian; as it circles
the earth, passes over a track of infamy, of outrage, of carnage
and of blood. The London *Times*, speaking of Ireland, says
that "man is a drug, and population a nuisance."

> Like Banquo's ghost see Emmet's spirit rise
> And shake its gory locks at her, while she
> "Avaunt! Avaunt!" like Macbeth vainly cries,
> And would but cannot flee.

Returning from Moscow and St. Petersburg I passed
through Sweden and Norway, and here I listened to the tales
of the departed. I seemed to feel the presence of the Mael-
strom. What causes that terrible pool? Where does the
water drop to? Is there another world below? I have
seen birds and animals that have been forced over the falls
at Niagara by the rushing of the waters; but how feeble is
that compared to the power that draws in both the little and
the great? Whales from afar off are spirited into the cave

and it is fatal to any ship that wanders too close to its whirl-
ing eddies. I should like to take a look into that subterra-
nean cavern. What skeletons! What history! Has Lord
Palmerston organized a whirlpool for the Irish members of
Parliament? Humanity is weak. See how the men of the
day are drawn into the stream. The whirlpool is now
almost as large as that of Norway, and the skeletons of good
men and honest men are packed along the cavern almost as
thick as in the city of the dead, or the field of a hundred
battles. The sexagenarians, septugenarians and octogenari-
ans, comprising the English minority, cannot much longer
fool the English people and Irish laborer by making England
a pastorage and Ireland a desert for the aristocracy (of Sir
John Villiers Shelly's stamp) by taxing the people who they
always call the "mob." (Applause.)

HYPOCRISY IS HER GREAT RULE OF DIPLOMACY.

John Stuart Mill says, " an Englishman never feels safe unless he is living under the shadow of some legal fiction, on
agreement to say one thing and mean another."

Lying is her chief amusement, especially when she remains
neutral. [Laughter.] Jefferson once said that, " he never
found any general rule for foretelling what England would
do, but that of examining what she ought not to do."

The policy of England, said Gladstone (before he wished
his name removed from the Confederate loan list,) is, " trust
in the people tempered only by prudence, the policy of
England toward Ireland, is distrust of the people tempered
only by fear."

Ireland pensively mourns her lost children who're gone,
  Scattered broadcast on every shore ;
Some sleep in the deep, 'neath the wild waves alone,
  But these live to right her once more.
May Heaven pull down the cursed Saxon crown,
  That so long hath a gloom o'er her cast ;
And grant you once more a chance, on that shore,
  To take sweet revenge for the past.

England has copied, on a grand scale, the loathsome expedient of Augustus Cæsar for prolonging a worthless life. But
the Roman Emperor only ruined virgins, England destroys
nations. (Applause.) Ruskin calls England "a money-making
mob," and accuses the English nation of "despising literature,
despising science, despising art, despising nature, despising
compassion, and concentrating its soul on pence." (Laughter.)

Fenianism is not understood. It means liberty or death.
(Cheers.) The Order is older than the Roman. Here are its
Ten Commandments, taken from the Irish record before
Christendom : "Every soldier was required to swear that,
without regard to her fortune, he would choose a wife for her
virtue, her courtesy and her good manners; that he would
never offer violence to a woman ; that as far as he could he
would relieve the poor, and that he would not refuse to fight
nine men of any other nation. No person could be received
into the service unless his father and mother and all his rela-
tives gave security that none of them should avenge his death
upon the person who might slay him, but that they would
leave the matter to his fellow-soldiers. The youth himself
must be well acquainted with the twelve books of poetry, and
be able to compose verses. He must be a perfect master of
defense; to prove this, he was placed in a field of sedge reach-
ing up to his knees, having in his hands a target and a hazel
stick as long as a man's arm. Nine experienced soldiers,
from a distance of nine ridges of land, were to hurl their
spears at him at once ; if he was unhurt, he was admitted, but
if wounded he was sent off with a reproach. He must also

run well and defend himself when in fight; to try his activity
he was made to run through a wood, having a start of a tree's
breadth, the whole of the Fenians pursuing him; if he were
overtaken or wounded in the wood he was refused, as too
sluggish and unskillful to fight with honor among such valiant
troops.   Also, he must have a strong arm and be able to hold
his weapon steadily.   Also, when he ran through a wood in
chase his hair should not come untied; if it did he was rejected.   He must be so swift and light of foot as not to break a
rotten stick by standing upon it; able also to leap over a tree
as high as his forehead, and to stoop under a tree that was
lower than his knees.   Without stooping or lessening his
speed, he must be able to draw a thorn out of his foot.   Finally,
he must take an oath of fidelity to Ireland, and swear to die
for his wife, his child, his home, his country and his God.
(Loud cheers.)   That is Fenianism.

> Oh, let us pray to God, boys,
>   To grant the day, to grant the day,
> You may press your native sod, boys,
>   In linked array, in linked array!
> Let us give you arms and ships, boys,
>   You ask no more, you ask no more,
> And Ireland's long eclipse, boys,
>   Will soon be o'er, will soon be o'er.

This country must have American ideas, manufactures,
language, and a mother country of our own, says Andrew
Johnson.   (Loud cheers.)

England takes away our cotton, sends it across the seas to
her ports, transports it thirty miles to be manufactured, sends
it back in goods to clothe the Fenian Brotherhood.   [Shame
on America for allowing it.]   When England wants corn
make her pay gold for it.   Make laws that no cotton shall go
to her; send it out West to be worked up.   That will touch
her.   She has no heart or soul; you can only affect her
through her belly or her pocket.   [Loud laughter, and that's
so.]   In the Irish famine she repealed the duties on grain,

and the idiots here called it free trade. He was not for protection, he was for prohibition. He would not allow any
manufactured goods to be imported from England. Call
back our ambassadors from abroad, those who are listening
to sneers upon the country. They are not wanted there to
toady to the British aristocracy. Charles Francis Adams is
not an American. [That's so.] He referred to Bulwer's
dispatch to Palmerston, in 1851, as follows :

"The country is paralyzed by parties that do not think
there is any possibility of their uniting on any great internal
or external object. This of course paralyzes the Federal
power, if power it can be called, and leave you at liberty to
pursue to their consequences the project and advantages
which your lordship has conceded from our Central American
relations."

That was written from Washington by an English Embas-
sador, who was shortly afterward recalled for it.

The same letter said : "If the naturalized Irish ever adopt
an American platform, I cannot conceal from myself the
serious manner in which our American interests will be
jeopardized." This tells the story. This Fenian movement
is that Irish American platform referred to.

By this association you can be powerful. Pass resolutions
like the following :

1. *Resolved*, That the word English be unanimously
dropped, and that the words American language be used in
the future. (Loud cheers.)

2. *Resolved*, As America is twenty-one years of age, it is
time to establish a motherland of her own. (Applause.)

3. *Resolved*, That the one hundred millions of dollars due
for destroying our commerce shall be paid forthwith, or
England must take the consequences of American neutrality.
(Cheers and laughter.)

4. *Resolved*, That France is the friend of Ireland. Louis
Napoleon is not French. Every fifteen or twenty years there

is a revolution. They come regularly, and one will be along within two years.

In regard to the last resolution, the speaker argued that Louis Napoleon was not France, and that, ere long, in accordance with the decrees of a special fate which seems to have manifested itself in regard to every member of the Bonaparte family, he would cease to reign.

The question upon each of the above resolutions was taken as they were read, the vote being a unanimous "aye," and the result greeted with hearty cheers.

Mr. Train resumed: You have sounded the tocsin of revolution, and soon an outbreaking will spread throughout Europe. The two Napoleons had endeavored to draw the Popes from Rome. In answer to the first, the Pope had called him simply "Comedian" and "Tragedian," in reply to his passionate outbursts. Responding to the latter, the last Pope had called about him representatives from all the world of three hundred millions of Catholics. The revolutions come as regularly as clock work; one will come in 1867. "How are you, Mexico?"

He would say a few words about that. Mexico would prove the Moscow of Napoleon III. Napoleon will fall, and the republic will again come up in 1867. Have you ever observed the singular addition of figures foretelling the fall of a French dynasty? Here they are: 1794—Fall of the monarchy. 1815—Fall of Napoleon. 1830—Fall of the Elder Bourbon dynasty. 1842—Death of Duke of Orleans by fall from his horse, and hastening the revolution of '48. 1867—You can draw your own inference—Napoleon's dynasty will disappear that year. [Loud cheers.] The notice starts from Ireland, and will spread throughout Germany and France in two years.

England received an attack of apoplexy in the Crimean war. The second attack was that of American neutrality. The third will be her death through the Fenians. [Cheers.]

England is simply an *attache* of France; she drives the

coach, and Napoleon rides inside. He uses her as a catspaw
to draw the chestnuts out of the fire. She has obeyed all his
plans and designs. She fought the Russians and the Aus-
trians with France, as he wished. And now the head of the
Fenians is in the Tuilleries, planning for the future. [Cheers.]
It is with you, Irishmen, to follow out these promptings.

Some of your people may try to sell you out with British
gold. Thomas D'Arcey McGee [loud hisses] cannot be an
Irishman. A cuckoo must have laid him in the eagle's nest.
[Laughter and "that's so."]

Everything charmed my senses in the beautiful Island of
Joan. The land clove and the nutmeg, the tyre and the cas-
sowary, and sugar and coffee, and that most luscious of fruits,
the nangostine. But in this wonderful Garden of Eden there
is a tree of good and evil. Have you heard of the Upas
tree? It is no fable. Be careful how you approach it. The
poison reaches where the winds blow; nor tree, nor flower,
nor shrub can live within its influence. Birds drop dead as
they come within the circle, and animals and creeping things
are scattered among the dead. Each year the circle widens.
The air is heavy. What is the terrible secret? Inquire,
and death ensues. There is a Upas tree in England. What
magic influence has paralyzed the Irish members of Parliament? What is the matter with Mayune? Has *The Cork
Examiner* come too near, and has the Dublin paper been ex-
ploring in that vicinity? [Laughter.] Yes, your Upas is
the treasury. The sovereign fever freezes the blood. It
destroys morality, and truth meeteth it but to die. Like the
down on the peach, like the virtue of a woman, once lost
they never return again. So, once under the branches of the
Palmerston Upas tree, the soul of honor deadens, and men
become the miserable creeping things of tyranny and shame.
[Applause, and cries of "Shame!"]

Your ancestors, so glorious in the eye of the world; so
bountiful and magnificent to their country; so sparing, so
modest, so self-denying to themselves--what resemblance can

we find, in the present generation (of Englishmen), to these great men?

Do you recognize the language?

It is the scorching sarcasm of Demosthenes, when rousing up the Athenians. [Cheers.]

You can say to the rulers of Ireland: You lavish the public money in scandalous and obscene uses; you suffer your allies to perish in time of peace, whom you preserved in time of war; and your mercenary court, and servile resignation to the will and pleasure of designing, insidious ministers, abet, encourage, and strengthen the most dangerous and formidable of your enemies. [Shame.]

Do you recognize the language? Demosthenes is exciting the people against Philip.

Cast your eye upon the magistrate (Lord Palmerston) under whose ministry you boast these precious improvements (in Ireland.) Behold him raised all at once from poverty to opulence; from the lowest obscurity to the highest honors. Look at his followers. Have not some of these upstarts built private houses and seats vieing with the most sumptuous of public palaces? And how have their fortunes and their power increased but as Ireland has been ruined and impoverished. (That's so.)

Do you recognize the language?

The orator was in Athens, and Phillip was the mark he fired at.

Why all this—Demosthenes is always eloquent.

The servant is now become the master. The magistrate was then subservient to the people; punishments and rewards were properties of the people; all honors, dignities and preferment were disposed by the voice and favor of the people; but the magistrate has now usurped the rights of the people, and exercises an abiding authority over his natural master. (Applause.)

Do you recognize the language?

Athens groaned under the biting rebukes of the eloquent Athenian, as Ireland is groaning now under English tyranny. But I have forgotten my resolutions. (Laughter.) Here are the others.

5. *Resolved,* That Ireland is a belligerent. That America (as England did in our civil war) should remain strictly neutral, while our merchants and bankers, our Lairds and Lindsays, fit out one hundred Sumters, Alabamas and Shenandoahs to sweep the commerce of England from the ocean, as England has done American commerce.

6. And last. *Resolved,* That as England has shown neither soul, or heart, or humanity in our rebellion, and can only be reached through the belly and pocket, that we, the Fenian Brotherhood and Sisterhood, will never use any article of English manufacture. We do not want protection, but prohibition.

The two preceding resolutions were adopted with loud exclamations of delight. (The audience again rising and making the building shake with their cheers.)

Andrew Jackson said the Union must and shall be preserved. Andrew Johnson says the Union must and shall be restored.

Wendell Phillips said we must have universal suffrage, or repudiation of the national debt. Afterward he repudiated his words though one thousand persons heard him. He made an assertion and backed down. I will make one which I will hold fast to. Stop talking negro suffrage or the Northern Democratic vote will unite with the Southern vote and repudiate.

BREAKERS AHEAD—TRAIN ON FINANCE.

Formerly three hundred millions of currency inflated markets, and everything went kiting. Latterly three thousand

millions of currency, and everything stagnates! What means
this apathy? Our large merchants are all short. There
were never so many borrowers. Our large bankers appear
to be flush—money never was so plenty. But long loans
don't take. Everybody loans on call; hence money is used
from hand to mouth. Nobody has confidence. No foundries
building—no ships on the stocks—no factories going up—no
new dwellings of consequence—no industrial enterprises
under way—and yet three thousand millions of currency.
What does it mean? The negro suffrage party want to add
seven hundred thousand votes to the suffrage. Will these
new votes, added to the white Southern vote, willingly be
thrown for taxation? (No.) Will they pay Northern debt
taxation without a murmur when they have lost almost
everything? Again, will the working men's vote, say one
million four hundred thousand, out of the one million eight
hundred thousand, go for taxation when they do not hold
any of the bonds? (No, unless they stop Southern niggers.)
Are these questions by germinating in the public mind
occasioning this strange apathy? Again, our bonds abroad
are at 70. They may go higher. Already $400,000,000 are
held in Europe—one-seventh the whole—interest payable in
gold. Suppose they continue buying as evidently, if paid, it
is the best investment in the world. Suppose they buy—
$1,000,000,000,—six per cent. is $60,000,000 in gold. Shall
we dig out that much? Suppose free trade becomes popular,
repudiation is certain. It may be this that causes the strange
apathy. If we are solvent, England buys our bonds, and we
import $150,000,000 more than we export. Gold will go to
200 before Congress adjourns. Would money be long with
the banker if they were obliged to redeem anything? That
is the question. This is my conviction which I will not
repudiate. The loyal leaguers must still be blackguarding
the South and talking negro suffrage, or three millions of
votes will be thrown in 1868 to wipe out the debt. (Loud
applause.)

Mind what I say—I believe in keeping sacred the national honor. But I think it is necessary to, do something to frighten Europe from buying our bonds and the fanatics from debasing our franchise. I am willing that education should be the test. The debt is only safe by keeping it at home. Something must be done for the South before they will vote to be taxed for their destruction.

The *Evening Post*, an English journal, without one particle of American feeling in its composition, says under

A LITTLE MORE NONSENSE.

A morning journal reports that the rise in the price of printing paper is disturbing the minds of the people in those official bureaus at Washington where it is used and supplied : and it is asserted that " the Treasury authorities are considering a project of building a Government paper mill at Great Falls on the Potomac." Does it not occur to these people that a cheaper and quicker way is to take the duty off foreign paper ? That will make paper cheap, not merely to the Government but to the people.

Here is toadyism that will destroy this nation. England praised Thanatropsis a generation or two ago, and Bryant has sworn by English Exeter Hall and English Free Trade Hall ever since. Just think for a moment of an American newspaper advising the Government to have the notes on which their bonds are printed, manufactured in England. [Shame.]

That is toadyism with a vengeance. French mission on the brain has destroyed the independence of the New York press. [Laughter.]

THE DAILY NEWS.

The Daily News is the only journal there that has preached the Sermon on the Mount. Although at one time I belonged to the church militant and opposed *The News'* policy, I now am a member of the church triumphant. *The News*, by helping me to break up Chicago, did more to elect Johnson than all the Abolition papers in the country, and was the first, to publish all your Fenian meetings. [Loud cheers.] The Fenian Brotherhood will never buy *The World*; they have voted down all articles of English manufacture. [Laughter.]

The whole Atlantic Ocean is paved with the skulls of negroes whom Englishmen threw overboard trying to introduce slavery into our country. [That's so.] He was opposed to negro suffrage. He was for the rights of the white man, not the black man. England has four hundred million dollars of our bonds, for which in twelve years we must pay three times that amount. We must stop this going abroad or we will be ruined. We had better attend to this matter and let the negroes alone. We must respect the rights of the white man. We have been talking negro ever since I was born. By killing slavery they have destroyed the slave. Read my discussion with Cassius M. Clay three years ago, and the *London Times'* editorial thereon. I told them that I did not wish to see the poor negro destroyed.

ONE MORE LIE NAILED.

The *London Morning Post*, Lord Palmerston's organ, says: "The designs of the conspirators," as stated by the counsel for the crown, "partook of the character of socialism in the most vicious and dangerous shape. The lower classes were led to expect a redistribution of the property of the country, and that any man who possessed more property than another had an advantage over his fellows, which should not be permitted. The operations of this revolution were to commence by the indiscriminate massacre and assassination of all those above the lower classes, including the Roman Catholic clergymen, against whom their animosity is particularly directed for their opposition to the views of the brotherhood." Such was the end and object of this so-called national movement in Ireland, which we are assured by Mr. Barry will be proved on the trial to have been "manifested in writings, both public and private," which will be brought home to the accused.

I pronounce that a malicious lie. [Cheers.] The Irish are not assassins. The Irish did not build pirate ships to run the blockade. The Irish did not call American soldiers fools, ninnies and tailors. The Irish did not bombard Copenhagen, and then some generations later let their Prince Regent marry a Danish Princess, and then sell out the Danes to the highest bidder, as England did in the Schleswig Holstein affair. [Applause.] Did the Prince of Wales find something sound at last in Denmark? Hamlet would not have treated his sister so. Did the Irish tie Sepoy soldiers on English cannon and fire them off for amusement? [Shame and groans for England.] The counsel for the crown has lied when he calls the Irish assassins. England cannot tell the truth. There is no law for the poor; their trial by jury is a farce. I remember a case where one Sir John Villiers Shelley openly insulted every woman in England in the Queen's drawing room, yet because a poor landlord brought the charge, Lord Lanover told the corrupt Judge that it must be an illusion. [Laughter.] The Onanized Baronet, however, has at last been kicked out of Westminster, to make room for John Stuart Mill, as well as kicked out of English society, yet *The Times* censured me and cleared the member of Parliament. Shelley and Lord Campbell own largely in *The Times*. Did they get some of the Confederate loan? Beresford Hope (*Saturday Review* proprietor), denies losing. So does Delané, and *Morning Post.* Hope is the eye glared snob who called Seward an unprincipled knave, and Lincoln an incapable pretender. I remember his once testifying before Judge Yardly that the flange of the Bayswater Street Rail was a foot and half wide. [Loud laughter.]

The English press are in the witness box, and we have got them tight—a palpable hit. They squirm. They deny—but nobody doubts their guilt. They say they have not lost. Of course not. We, Wall street people, always put down so much in the stock to the money writer. If it goes up he makes. If it goes down he loses nothing. The same was done in London. Mason made the arrangement when I was in St. James street. The list is correct as it stands, as can be proved from the Southern archives.

. We who have been treated so badly by England wish to take the right position in regard to neutrality. Be organized; let your movement be no failure. Ireland has not to-day all the Irishmen. Tens of thousands are in the streets of London. Beneath many an English coat you will find an Irish heart. All through England revolution is ripe. Thousands of workingmen will aid you. More will fight for you than will fight against you.

I spoke four years ago to an excited audience in London of the Sons of Saint Patrick. The Downfall of England speech was copied all over the world. Shortly afterward I was in jail; they said for debt; yet I had twenty thousand pounds in the hands of my English bankers at the time. [Applause.] And some of those bankers who did the fiddling will have to pay the fiddler. [Laughter.] Mr. John O'Mahony must stop the howling of the English press. Turning to Mr. Roberts, the Chairman and President of the Central Council, Mr. Train said, Why don't you send over two hundred thousand dollars in the bonds of the Irish Republic and divide them among the London newspapers? [Laughter and applause.]

Then they will swear by Ireland as they did by the Confederate Government. [Laughter and "That's so."]

In conclusion let me advise you when you vote again to abolish all State sovereignty, Monroe doctrine and free trade absurdities; abolish bribes to Presidents; abolish Electoral College policy, and open the President to election from the people; [cheers;] abolish Ministers to foreign Courts, and establish commercial agents instead.

Establish Father Mathew societies under the leadership of my friend Carey here in every town. Shake hands with the clergy, who are really with you at heart [cheers], although some of them have opposed your organization. Educate your children to love God, love truth, love virtue, and be happy. [Applause.] Avoid the rum shop as you would the plague—[laughter]—and leave American women to drink whisky under the scoundrelly advice of the family doctor— and American young men to get the delirium tremens by loafing around the bars of our hotels—but don't let it be said that Irishmen are drunkards. No drunkard can belong to the F. B. [Applause]. Swear by Andrew Johnson. [Cheers.] The Radicals intend to impeach him this winter. Elect your own members of Congress, and cry Ireland for the Irish. [Loud cheers.]

> Ye sons of liberty arise,
> Your hearths and altars are at stake,
> Arise! arise! for freedom's sake,
> And strike with John O'Mahony.

(Loud applause.)

> Your Irish eagle is not dead,
> Again his Irish wings are spread
> To sweep upon old England's head,
> And strike with John O'Mahony.

(Loud cheers.)

> What soul but scorns the cursed slave?
> Oh! liberty is for the brave;
> Your cry be Ireland or the grave,
> And on with John O'Mahony.

(Loud and continued applause, the entire Circle on the stage rising with the audience to cheers proposed for Mr. Train, Mr. Seward, the President, and others.)

Mr. Train having spoken for two hours, he withdrew, when some of the Fenian orators came to time, and eloquent speeches were made by Col. Roberts of New York, Hine and Powers of Massachusetts, Knight of Ohio, Gibbon, head Center for Pennsylvania, Mr. Walsh, Gen. Sweeny, McDermott and others. The Philadelphia press was fully represented on the stage.

The meeting was, in every respect, a great success to Mr. Train and the Irish cause, to which the proceeds were all given.

THE END.

T. B. PETERSON & BROTHERS' PUBLICATIONS.

THIS CATALOGUE CONTAINS AND
Describes the Most Popular and Best Selling Books in the World
NEW BOOKS ISSUED EVERY WEEK,

Comprising the most entertaining and absorbing works published, suitable for the Parlor, Library, Sitting Room, Railroad, Steamboat or Soldiers' reading, by the best writers in the world.

Published and for Sale by T. B. PETERSON & BROTHERS, Philad'a.

☞ Booksellers and all others will be Supplied at very Low Rates. ☜

☞ TERMS : To those with whom we have no monthly account, Cash with Order. ☜

MRS. SOUTHWORTH'S WORKS.

Tried for her Life. One volume, paper cover. Price 1.50 ; or in one volume, cloth, for $2.00.

The Bridal Eve. Complete in one volume, paper cover. Price $1.50 ; or in one volume, cloth,$2.00.

The Fatal Marriage. Complete in one volume, paper cover. Price $1.50 ; or in one vol., cloth, $2.00.

Love's Labor Won. One volume, paper cover, Price $1.50 ; or in one volume, cloth, for $2.00.

The Gipsy's Prophecy. Complete in one vol., paper cover. Price $1.50 ; or in one vol., cloth, $2.00.

Vivia. The Secret of Power. One vol., paper cover. Price $1.50 ; or in one vol., cloth, $2.00.

India. The Pearl of Pearl River. One vol. paper cover. Price $1.50 ; or in cloth, $2.00.

Mother-in-Law. One volume, paper cover. Price $1.50 ; or in one volume, cloth, for $2.00.

The Two Sisters. One volume, paper cover. Price $1.50 ; or in one volume, cloth, for $2.00.

The Three Beauties. One volume, paper cover. Price $1.50 ; or in one volume, cloth, for $2.00.

The Wife's Victory. One volume, paper cover. Price $1.50 ; or in one volume, cloth, for $2.00.

The Lost Heiress. One volume, paper cover. Price $1.50 ; or in one volume, cloth, for $2.00.

The Deserted Wife. One volume, paper cover. Price $1.50 ; or in one volume, cloth, for $2.00.

The Lady of the Isle. Complete in one vol., paper cover. Price $1.50 ; or in one vol., cloth, $2.00.

The Missing Bride. One volume, paper cover. Price $1.50 ; or in one volume, cloth, for $2.00.

Retribution: A Tale of Passion. One vol., paper cover. Price $1.50 ; or in one vol., cloth, $2.00.

The Haunted Homestead. One volume, paper cover. Price $1.50 ; or in one volume, cloth, $2.00.

The Curse of Clifton. One volume, paper cover. Price $1.50 ; or in one volume, cloth, for $2.00.

The Discarded Daughter. One vol., paper cover. Price $1.50 ; or in one volume, cloth, for $2.00.

Hickory Hall. By Mrs.Southworth. Price 50 cents.

The Broken Engagement. Price 25 cents.

The Jealous Husband. One volume, paper cover. Price $1.50 ; or in one volume, cloth, for $2.00.

The Belle of Washington. One vol., paper cover. Price $1.50 ; or in one volume, cloth, for $2.00.

The Initials. A Love Story. One vol., paper cover. Price $1.50 ; or in one volume, cloth, $2.00.

Family Secrets. One volume, paper cover. Price $1.50 ; or bound in one volume, cloth, for $2.00.

Self-Sacrifice. One volume, paper cover. Price $1.50 ; or in one volume, cloth, for $2 00.

Courtship and Matrimony. One vol., paper cover. Price $1.50 ; or in one vol., cloth, $2.00.

High Life in Washington. One vol., paper cover. Price $1.50 ; or in one vol., cloth, $2.00.

The Woman in Black. One vol., paper cover. Price $1.50 ; or bound in one volume, cloth, for $2.00.

Family Pride. One volume, paper cover. Price $1.50 ; or bound in one volume, cloth, for $2.00.

The Lovers Trials. One vol., paper cover. Price $1.50 ; or in one vol., cloth, for $2.00.

Rose Douglas. One volume, paper cover. Price $1.50 ; or bound in one volume, cloth, for $2.00.

MRS. ANN S. STEPHENS' WORKS.

Silent Struggles. One volume, paper cover Price $1.50 ; or in one volume, cloth, $2.00.

The Wife's Secret. One volume, paper cover. Price $1.50 ; or in one volume, cloth, for $2.00

The Rejected Wife. One volume, paper cover. Price $1.50 ; or bound in one volume, cloth, for 2.00.

Fashion and Famine. One volume, paper cover. Price $1.50 ; or bound in one vol., cloth, $2.00.

The Heiress. One volume, paper cover. Price $1.50 ; or bound in one volume, cloth, for $2.00.

The Old Homestead. One volume, paper cover. Price $1.50 ; or bound in one volume, cloth, for $2 00.

Mary Derwent. One volume, paper cover. Price $1.50 ; or bound in one vol., cloth, for $2.00.

CAROLINE LEE HENTZ'S WORKS.

Planter's Northern Bride. One vol., paper cover. Price $1.50 ; or in one vol., cloth, for $2.00.

Linda. The Young Pilot of the Belle Creole. Price $1.50 in paper ; or $2.00 in cloth.

Robert Graham. The Sequel to, and Continuation of Linda. Price $1.50 in paper ; or $2.00 in cloth

The Lost Daughter. One vol., paper cover. Price $1.50 ; or bound in one volume, cloth, for $2.00.

Courtship and Marriage. One vol., paper cover. Price $1.50 ; or in one volume, cloth, for $2.00

Rena; or, The Snow Bird. One vol., paper cover. Price $1.50 ; or in one vol., cloth, for $2.00.

Marcus Warland. One volume, paper cover. Price $1.50 ; or bound in one vol., cloth, for $2.00.

Love after Marriage. One vol., paper cover. Price $1.50 ; or bound in one volume, cloth, for $2.00.

The Planter's Daughter. One vol., paper cover. Price $1.50 ; or bound in one vol., cloth, $2.00

Eoline; or, Magnolia Vale. One vol., paper cover. Price $1.50 ; or in one vol., cloth, $2.00.

The Banished Son. One volume, paper cover. Price $1.50 ; or bound in one volume, cloth, $2.00.

Helen and Arthur. One volume, paper cover. Price $1.50 ; or bound in one volume, cloth, $2.00.

Earnest Linwood. One volume, paper cover. Price $1.50 ; or bound in one vol., cloth, for $2.00.

Forsaken Daughter. One volume, paper cover. Price $1.50 ; or in one volume, cloth, $2.00.

Beautiful Widow. One volume, paper cover. Price $1.50 ; or in one volume, cloth, $2.00.

Brother's Secret. One volume, paper cover Price $1.50 ; or in one volume, cloth, $2.00.

The Matchmaker. One volume, paper cover Price $1.50 ; or in one volume, cloth, $2.00.

SINCLAIR'S, LADY SCOTT'S : ETC.

Flirtations in Fashionable Life. One vol. paper cover. Price $1.50 ; or in one vol., cloth, $2.00.

The Pride of Life. One volume, paper cover. Price $1.50 ; or bound in one volume, cloth, for $2.00.

The Rival Belles. One volume, paper cover Price $1.50 ; or in one volume, cloth, for $2.00.

The Devoted Bride. One volume.

Love and Duty. One volume.

The Lost Love. One volume

The Bohemians of London. One volume.

Price of above $1.50 in paper ; or $2 in cloth.

CAPTAIN MARRYATT'S WORKS.
Price Fifty cents each.

Japhet in Search of a Father.
Snarleyow.
   The King's Own.
Newton Foster.
   Pirate and Three Cutters.
Phantom Ship.
Jacob Faithful.
   The Naval Officer.
     Pacha of Many Tales.
     Midshipman Easy. .
Percival Keene.
Peter Simple.
   Sea King.
   Poor Jack.

CHARLES DICKENS' WORKS.
ILLUSTRATED OCTAVO EDITION. ·
Each book being complete in one volume.

Our Mutual Friend,	Cloth,	$2.50
Pickwick Papers,	Cloth,	2.50
Nicholas Nickleby,	Cloth,	2.50
Great Expectations,	Cloth,	2.50
Lamplighter's Story,	Cloth,	2.50
Oliver Twist,	Cloth,	2.50
Bleak House,	Cloth,	2.50
Little Dorrit,	Cloth,	2.50
Dombey and Son,	Cloth,	2.50
Sketches by "Boz,"	Cloth,	2.50
David Copperfield,	Cloth,	2.50
Barnaby Rudge,	Cloth,	2.50
Martin Chuzzlewit,	Cloth,	2.50
Old Curiosity Shop,	Cloth,	2.50
Christmas Stories,	Cloth,	2.50
Dickens' New Stories,	Cloth,	2.50
A Tale of Two Cities,	Cloth,	2.50
American Notes and Pic-Nic Papers.		2.50

Price of a set, in Black cloth, in 18 volumes........$44.00
"   "   Full Law Library style............ 53.00
"   "   Half calf, sprinkled edges........ 63.00
"   "   Half calf, marbled edges.. .... 68.00
"   "   Half calf, antique 78.00
"   "   Half calf, full gilt backs, etc..... 78.00

PEOPLE'S DUODECIMO EDITION.
Each book being complete in one volume.

Our Mutual Friend,	Cloth,	$2.00
Pickwick Papers,	Cloth,	2.00
Nicholas Nickleby,	Cloth,	2.00
Great Expectations,	Cloth,	2.00
Lamplighter's Story,	Cloth,	2.00
David Copperfield,	Cloth,	2.00
Oliver Twist,	Cloth,	2.00
Bleak House,	Cloth,	2.00
A Tale of Two Cities,	Cloth,	2.00
Dickens' New Stories,	Cloth,	2.00
Little Dorrit,	Cloth,	2.00
Dombey and Son,	Cloth,	2.00
Christmas Stories,	Cloth,	2.00
Sketches by "Boz,"	Cloth,	2.00
Barnaby Rudge,	Cloth,	2.00
Martin Chuzzlewit,	Cloth,	2.00
Old Curiosity Shop,	Cloth,	2.00
Dickens' Short Stories,	Cloth,	2.00
Message from the Sea,	Cloth,	2.00

Price of a set, in Black cloth, in 18 volumes......$36.00
"   "   Full Law Library style.......... 44.00
"   "   Half calf, sprinkled edges....... 58.00
"   "   Half calf, marbled edges.. ...... 63.00
"   "   Half calf, antique 72.00
"   "   Half calf, full gilt backs, etc..... 72.00

CHARLES DICKENS' WORKS.
ILLUSTRATED DUODECIMO EDITION.
Each book being complete in two volumes.

Our Mutual Friend.	Cloth,	$4.00
Pickwick Papers,	Cloth,	4.00
Tale of Two Cities,	Cloth,	4.00
Nicholas Nickleby,	Cloth,	4.00
David Copperfield,	Cloth,	4.00
Oliver Twist,	Cloth,	4.00
Christmas Stories,	Cloth,	4.00
Bleak House,	Cloth,	4.00
Sketches by "Boz,"	Cloth,	4.00
Barnaby Rudge,	Cloth,	4.00 '
Martin Chuzzlewit,	Cloth,	4.00
Old Curiosity Shop,	Cloth,	4.00
Little Dorrit,	Cloth,	4.00
Dombey and Son,	Cloth,	4.00

The following are each complete in one volume.

Great Expectations,	Cloth,	2.00
Lamplighter's Story,	Cloth,	2.00
Dickens' New Stories,	Cloth,	2.00
Message from the Sea,	Cloth,	2.00

Price of a set, in 32 vols. bound in cloth, gilt backs $84.00
"   "   Full Law Library style............ 80.00
"   "   Half calf, antique 125.00
"   "   Half calf, full gilt back..........125.00

CHARLES DICKENS' WORKS.
CHEAP EDITION, PAPER COVER.
Price Seventy-five cents a volume.

Pickwick Papers.
   Great Expectations.
     A Tale of Two Cities.
       New Years' Stories.
         Barnaby Rudge.
           Old Curiosity Shop.
Little Dorrit.
   David Copperfield.
     Sketches by "Boz."
       Dickens' New Stories.
         American Notes.
Oliver Twist.
   Lamplighter's Story.
     Dombey and Son.
       Nicholas Nickleby.
         Holiday Stories.
           Martin Chuzzlewit.
Bleak House.
   Dickens' Short Stories.
     Message from the Sea.
       Christmas Stories.
         Pic-Nic Papers.
Our Mutual Friend. Illustrated. Price $1.00.
Christmas Carols. Price 25 cents.
Somebody's Luggage. Price 25 cents.
Tom Tiddler's Ground. Price 25 cents.
The Haunted House. Price 25 cents.

LIBRARY OCTAVO EDITION, IN NINE VOLS.

(A New Edition in Press.)

This edition is in NINE large octavo volumes, with a Portrait of Charles Dickens, and contains his complete writings, profusely illustrated, and bound in the following various styles.

Price of a set, in Black Cloth, in nine volumes,..$26.00
"   "   Law Library style,.............. 31.00
"   "   Half calf, sprinkled edges,...... 33.00
"   "   Half calf, marbled edges,........ 36.00
"   "   Half calf, antique,.............. 45.00
"   "   Half calf, full gilt backs, etc..... 45.00

CHARLES LEVER'S WORKS.

Fine Edition, bound separately.

Charles O'Malley, cloth,............................	$2.00
Harry Lorrequer, cloth	2.00
Jack Hinton, cloth, ...	2.00
Davenport Dunn, cloth,............................	2.00
Tom Burke of Ours, cloth,......................	2.00
Arthur O'Leary, cloth	2.00
Con Cregan, cloth.................................	2.00
Knight of Gwynne, cloth, ...	2.00
Valentine Vox, cloth,.............................	2.00
Ten Thousand a Year, cloth,.....	2.00

CHARLES LEVER'S NOVELS.

All neatly done up in paper covers.

Charles O'Malley,........................	Price 75	cts.
Harry Lorrequer,...........................	75	"
Horace Templeton,........................	75	"
Tom Burke of Ours,.....................	75	"
Jack Hinton, the Guardsman,...	75	"
Arthur O'Leary,...........................	75	"
The Knight of Gwynne,................	75	"
Kate O'Donoghue,......................	75	"
Con Cregan, the Irish Gil Blas, ...	75	"
Davenport Dunn,..........................	75	"
Valentine Vox,.............................	75	"
Diary of a Medical Student.............	75	"

LIBRARY EDITION.

THIS EDITION is complete in FIVE large octavo volumes, containing Charles O'Malley, Harry Lorrequer, Horace Templeton, Tom Burke of Ours, Arthur O'Leary, Jack Hinton the Guardsman, The Knight of Gwynne, Kate O'Donoghue, etc., handsomely printed, and bound in various styles, as follows:

Price of a set in Black cloth,....................	$10.00
" Scarlet cloth,..........	11.00
" " Law, Library sheep,..........	12.50
" " Half Calf, sprinkled edges,........	16.50
" " Half Calf, marbled edges,........	17.00
" " Half Calf, antique, ...	20.00

WILKIE COLLINS' GREAT WORKS.

The Dead Secret. One volume, octavo. Price 75 cents; or bound in one vol., cloth, for $1.00; or a fine 12mo. edition, in one vol., paper cover, in large type, for $1.50, or in one vol., cloth, for $2.00.

The Crossed Path; or, Basil. Complete in one volume, paper cover. Price $1.50, or bound in one volume, cloth, for $2.00.

Hide and Seek. One vol., octavo, paper cover. Price 75 cents; or bound in one vol., cloth, for $1.00.

After Dark. One vol., octavo, paper cover. Price 75 cents; or bound in one vol., cloth, for $1.00.

Sights a-foot; or Travels Beyond Railways. One volume, octavo, paper cover. Price 50 cents.

The Yellow Mask. Price 25 cents.

The Stolen Mask. Price 25 cents.

Sister Rose. Price 25 cents.

MISS PARDOE'S WORKS.

Confessions of a Pretty Woman. By Miss Pardoe. Complete in one volume. Price 75 cents.

The Jealous Wife. By Miss Pardoe. Complete in one large octavo volume. Price Fifty cents.

The Wife's Trials. By Miss Pardoe. Complete in one large octavo volume. Price 75 cents.

The Rival Beauties. By Miss Pardoe. Complete in one large octavo volume. Price 75 cents.

Romance of the Harem. By Miss Pardoe. Complete in one large octavo vol. Price Fifty cents.

Miss Pardoe's Complete Works. This comprises the whole of the above Five works, and are bound in cloth, gilt, in one volume. Price $4.00.

The Adopted Heir. By Miss Pardoe. One vol., paper. Price $1.50; or in one vol., cloth, for $2.00.

A Life's Struggle. Cloth. Price $2.00.

COOK BOOKS.

Mrs. Goodfellow's Cookery as it should be. A New Manual of the Dining Room and Kitchen. Price $2.00.

Petersons' New Cook Book; or Useful Receipts for the Housewife and the uninitiated. One vol., bound. Price $2.00.

Miss Leslie's New Cookery Book. Being her last new book. One volume, bound. Price $2.00.

Widdifield's New Cook Book; or, Practical Receipts for the Housewife. Cloth. Price $2.00.

Mrs. Hale's New Cook Book. By Mrs. Sarah J. Hale. One volume, bound. Price $2.00.

Miss Leslie's New Receipts for Cooking Complete in one volume, bound. Price $2.00.

MRS. HALE'S RECEIPTS.

Mrs. Hale's Receipts for the Million. Containing 4545 Receipts. By Mrs. Sarah J. Hale. One vol., 800 pages, strongly bound. Price $2 00.

FRANCATELLI'S FRENCH COOK.

Francatelli's Celebrated French Cook Book. The Modern Cook. A Practical Guide to the Culinary Art, in all its branches; comprising, in addition to English Cookery, the most approved and recherché systems of French, Italian, and German Cookery; adapted as well for the largest establishments, as for the use of private families. By CHARLES ELME FRANCATELLI, pupil to the celebrated CAREME, and late Maitre-d'Hôtel and Chief Cook to her Majesty, the Queen of England. With Sixty-Two Illustrations of various dishes. Complete in one large octavo volume of Six Hundred pages. Price $5.00.

SAMUEL C. WARREN'S BOOKS.

Ten Thousand a Year. Complete in one vol., paper cover. Price $1.50; or an edition, in one volume, cloth, for $2.00.

Diary of a Medical Student. By author of "Ten Thousand a Year." Complete in one octavo volume, paper cover. Price 75 cents.

EMERSON BENNETT'S WORKS.

The Border Rover. Fine edition, bound in cloth, for $2.00; or Railroad Edition for $1.50.

Clara Moreland. Fine edition, bound in cloth, for $2.00; or Railroad Edition, in paper, for $1.50.

The Forged Will. Fine edition, bound in cloth, for $2.00; or Railroad Edition, in paper, for $1.50.

Ellen Norbury. Fine edition, bound in cloth, for $2.00; or Railroad Edition, in paper, for $1.50.

Bride of the Wilderness. Fine edition, bound in cloth, for $2.00; or Railroad Edition for $1.50.

Kate Clarendon. Fine edition, bound in cloth, for $2.00; or Railroad Edition, in paper, for $1.50.

Viola. Fine edition, cloth, for $2.00; or Railroad Edition for $1.50.

Heiress of Bellefonte and Walde-Warren. Price 50 cents.

Pioneer's Daughter; and the Unknown Countess. Price 50 cents.

W. H. MAXWELL'S WORKS.

Stories of Waterloo. One of the best books in the English language. One vol. Price 75 cents.

Brian O'Lynn; or, Luck is Everything. 75 cents.

Wild Sports in the West. Price 75 cents.

DOESTICKS' BOOKS.

Doesticks' Letters. Complete in one volume, paper cover. Price $1.50; or in one vol., cloth, $2.00.

Plu-ri-bus-tah. Complete in one vol., paper cover. Price $1.50; or in one vol., cloth, $2.00.

The Elephant Club. Complete in one vol., paper cover. Price $1.50; or in one vol., cloth, $2.00.

Witches of New York. Complete in one vol., paper cover. Price $1.50; or in one vol., cloth, $2.00.

Nothing to Say. Illustrated. Price 75 cents.

Copies of any of the above Works will be sent, Free of Postage, on Receipt of Retail Price,
By T. B. PETERSON & BROTHERS, Philadelphia, Pa.

MRS. HENRY WOOD'S BOOKS.

Mildred Arkell. One volume, paper cover. Price $1.50; or in cloth, $2.00.

Lord Oakburn's Daughters; or, Earl's Heirs. One volume, paper cover. Price $1.50; or in cloth, $2.00.

Oswald Cray. One volume, paper cover. Price $1.50; or in one volume, cloth, for $2.00.

The Shadow of Ashlydyat. One vol., paper cover. Price $1.50; or in one vol., cloth, for $2.00.

Squire Trevlyn's Heir; or, Trevlyn Hold. One vol., paper cover. Price $1.50; or in one volume, cloth, for $2.00.

The Castle's Heir. One vol., octavo, paper cover. Price $1.50; or in one volume, cloth, for $2.00.

Verner's Pride. One vol., octavo, paper cover. Price $1.50; or bound in one vol., cloth, for $2.00.

The Channings. One volume, octavo, paper cover. Price $1.00; or in one vol., cloth, for $1.50.

The Red Court Farm. Price 75 cents.

A Life's Secret. One volume, paper cover. Price Fifty cents; or bound in one volume, cloth, for $1.00.

The Mystery. Paper, 75 cents; or in cloth, $1.00.

The Lost Bank Note. Price 75 cents.

The Haunted Tower. Price Fifty cents.

The Lost Will; or, The Diamond Bracelet. Price 50 cents.

The Runaway Match. One volume, paper cover. Price 50 cents.

Aurora Floyd. One volume, paper cover. Price 75 cents; or a finer edition, bound in cloth, for $1.50.

Better For Worse. One volume, octavo, paper cover. Price 75 cents.

Foggy Night at Offord. Price 25 cents.

William Allair. One volume. Price 25 cents.

Lawyer's Secret. One volume. Price 25 cents.

ALEXANDER DUMAS' WORKS.

Count of Monte-Cristo. Illustrated. One volume, cloth, $2.00; or paper cover, for $1.50.

Edmond Dantes. Being a Sequel to Dumas' celebrated novel of the "Count of Monte-Cristo." 75 cts.

The Conscript. One vol., paper cover. Price $1.50; or in one vol., cloth, for $2.00.

Camille; or the Fate of a Coquette. Only correct Translation from the Original French. One volume, paper, price $1.50; or in cloth, $2.00.

The Three Guardsmen. Price 75 cents, in paper cover, or a finer edition in cloth for $2.00.

Twenty Years After. A Sequel to the "Three Guardsmen." Price 75 cents, in paper cover, or a finer edition, in one volume, cloth, for $2.00.

Bragelonne; the Son of Athos; being the continuation of "Twenty Years After." Price 75 cents, in paper, or a finer edition, in cloth, for $2.00.

The Iron Mask. Being the continuation of the "Three Guardsmen," "Twenty Years After," and "Bragelonne." Paper $1.00; or in cloth, $2.00.

Louise La Valliere; or, The Second Series and end of the "Iron Mask." Paper $1.00; or cloth, $2.

The Memoirs of a Physician. Beautifully Illustrated. Paper $1.00; or in cloth, for $2.00.

The Queen's Necklace; or, The "Second Series of the Memoirs of a Physician." Paper cover. Price $1.00; or in one vol., cloth, for $2.00.

Six Years Later; or, Taking of the Bastile. Being the "Third Series of the Memoirs of a Physician." Paper $1.00; or in cloth, for $2.00.

Countess of Charny; or, The Fall of the French Monarchy. Being the "Fourth Series of the Memoirs of a Physician." Paper $1.00; or in cloth, for $2.00.

Andree de Taverney. Being the "Fifth Series of the Memoirs of a Physician." Paper cover. Price $1.00; or in one vol., cloth, for $2.00.

The Chevalier; or, the "Sixth Series and final conclusion of the Memoirs of a Physician." Complete in one large octavo volume. Price $1.00.

The Adventures of a Marquis. Paper cover. Price $1.00; or in one vol. cloth for $2.00.

ALEXANDER DUMAS' WORKS.

The Forty-Five Guardsmen. Price 75 cts, or a finer edition in one volume, cloth. Price $2.00.

Diana of Meridor. Paper cover, Price One Dollar; or in one vol., cloth, for $2.00.

The Iron Hand. Price 75 cents, in paper cover, or a finer edition in one volume, cloth, for $2.00.

Annette; or, The Lady of the Pearls. A Companion to "Camille." Price 50 cents.

The Fallen Angel. A Story of Love and Life in Paris. One volume. Price 75 cents.

The Man with Five Wives. Complete in one volume. Price 75 cents.

George; or, The Planter of the Isle of France. One volume. Price Fifty cents.

The Mohicans of Paris. Price 50 cents.

Sketches in France. Price 75 cents.

Isabel of Bavaria. Price 75 cents.

Felina de Chambure; or, The Female Fiend. Price 75 cents.

The Horrors of Paris. Price 50 cents.

The Twin Lieutenants. Price 75 cents.

The Corsican Brothers. Price 25 cents.

FRANK E. SMEDLEY'S WORKS.

Harry Coverdale's Courtship and Marriage. One vol., paper. Price $1.50; or cloth, $2.00.

Lorrimer Littlegood. By author of "Frank Fairleigh." One vol., paper, price $1.50, or cloth 2.00.

Frank Fairleigh. One volume, cloth, $2.00; or cheap edition in paper cover, for 75 cents.

Lewis Arundel. One vol., cloth. Price $2.00; or cheap edition in paper cover, for 75 cents.

Fortunes and Misfortunes of Harry Racket Scapegrace. Cloth. Price $2.00; or cheap edition in paper cover, for 75 cents.

Tom Racquet; and His Three Maiden Aunts. Illustrated. Price 75 cents.

MRS. GREY'S NEW BOOKS.

Little Beauty. One vol., paper cover. Price $1.50; or in one volume, cloth, for $2.00.

Cousin Harry. One vol., paper cover. Price $1.50; or in one volume, cloth, for $2.00.

MRS. GREY'S POPULAR NOVELS.

Price Twenty-five cents each.

Alice Seymour. **Hyacinthe.**

Price Fifty cents each.

The Manœuvring Mother.
The Young Prima Donna.
The Gipsy's Daughter.
Belle of the Family.
Duke and Cousin.
The Little Wife.
Old Dower House.
Baronet's Daughters.
Sybil Lennard.
Lena Cameron.

Price Seventy-five cents each.

Passion & Principle.
Good Society.
Mary Seaham.
Lion Hearted.
The Flirt.

G. P. R. JAMES'S NEW BOOKS.

The Cavalier. An Historical Romance. With a steel portrait of the author. One vol., paper cover. Price $1.50; or in one vol., cloth, for $2.00.

Lord Montagu's Page. One volume, paper cover. Price $1.50; or in one vol., cloth, $2.00.

The Man in Black. Price 75 cents.

Arrah Neil. Price 75 cents.

Mary of Burgundy. Price 75 cents.

Eva St. Clair; and other Tales. Price 50 cents.

Copies of any of the above Works will be sent, Free of Postage, on Receipt of Retail Price
By T. B. PETERSON & BROTHERS, Philadelphia, Pa.

MILITARY NOVELS.

By Lever, Dumas, and other Authors.

With Illuminated Military Covers, in Colors, making them the most attractive and saleable books ever printed. Published and for sale at retail, by the single copy, or at wholesale, by the dozen, hundred, or thousand, at very low rates.

Their Names are as Follows :

Charles O'Malley	75
Jack Hinton, the Guardsman	75
The Knight of Gwynne	75
Harry Lorrequer	75
Tom Burke of Ours	75
Arthur O'Leary	75
Con Cregan's Adventures	75
Kate O Donoghue	75
Horace Templeton	75
Davenport Dunn	75
Valentine Vox	75
Twin Lieutenants	75
Stories of Waterloo	75
The Soldier's Wife	75
Tom Bowling's Adventures	75
Guerilla Chief	75
The Three Guardsmen	75
Jack Adams's Adventures,	75
Twenty Years After	75
Bragelonne, the Son of Athos	75
Wallace, Hero of Scotland	75
Forty-five Guardsmen	75
Life of Robert Bruce	75
The Gipsy Chief	75
Massacre of Glencoe	75
Life of Guy Fawkes	75
Child of Waterloo	75
Adventures of Ben Brace	75
Life of Jack Ariel	75
Following the Drum	50
The Conscript	1.50
Quaker Soldier, by Col. J. Richter Jones.	1.50

REYNOLDS' GREAT WORKS.

Mysteries of the Court of London. Complete in one large volume, bound in cloth, for $2.00; or in paper cover, price One Dollar.

Rose Foster; or, "The Second Series of the Mysteries of the Court of London." 1 vol., cloth, $2.50; or in paper cover, price $1.50.

Caroline of Brunswick ; or, the "Third Series of the Mysteries of the Court of London." Complete in one large vol., bound in cloth, for $2.00; or in paper cover, for $1.00.

Venetia Trelawney ; being the "Fourth Series, or final conclusion of the Mysteries of the Court of London." Complete in one large vol., in cloth, for $2.00; or in paper cover. Price $1.00.

Lord Saxondale ; or, The Court of Queen Victoria. Complete in one large vol., cloth, for $2.00; or in paper cover, price One Dollar.

Count Christoval. The "Sequel to Lord Saxondale." Complete in one vol., bound in cloth, for $2.00; or in paper cover, price $1.00.

The Necromancer. A Romance of the Times of Henry the Eighth. One vol., bound in cloth, for $2.00; or in paper cover, price $1.00.

Rosa Lambert ; or, The Memoirs of an Unfortunate Woman. One vol., bound in cloth, for $2.00; or in paper cover, price $1.00.

Mary Price ; or, The Adventures of a Servant-Maid. In one vol., cloth, for $2.00; or in paper $1.00.

Eustace Quentin. A "Sequel to Mary Price." In one vol., cloth, for $2.00; or in paper, $1.00.

Joseph Wilmot ; or, The Memoirs of a Man-Servant. In one vol., cloth, for $2.00; or in paper, $1.00.

REYNOLDS' GREAT WORKS.

The Banker's Daughter. A Sequel to "Joseph Wilmot." Complete in one vol., cloth for $2.00; or in paper cover, price $1.00.

Kenneth. A Romance of the Highlands. In one volume, cloth, for $2.00; or in paper, $1.00.

The Rye-House Plot ; or, Ruth, the Conspirator's Daughter. One vol., bound in cloth, for $2.00; or in paper cover, price One Dollar.

The Opera Dancer ; or, The Mysteries of London Life. Price 75 cents.

The Ruined Gamester. With Illustrations. Complete in one large octavo vol. Price Fifty cents.

Wallace: the Hero of Scotland. Illustrated with Thirty-eight plates. Price 75 cents.

The Child of Waterloo ; or, The Horrors of the Battle Field. Complete in one vol. Price 75 cents.

The Countess and the Page. Price 50 cents.

Ciprina ; or, The Secrets of a Picture Gallery. Complete in one vol. Price 50 cents.

Robert Bruce: the Hero King of Scotland, with his Portrait. One vol. Price 75 cents.

Isabella Vincent ; or, The Two Orphans. One volume, paper cover. Price 75 cents.

Vivian Bertram ; or, A Wife's Honor. A Sequel to "Isabella Vincent." One vol. Price 75 cents.

The Countess of Lascelles. The Continuation to "Vivian Bertram." One volume. Price 75 cents.

Duke of Marchmont. Being the Conclusion of "The Countess of Lascelles." Price 75 cents.

Gipsy Chief. Beautifully Illustrated. Complete in one large 8vo. volume. Price 75 cents.

Pickwick Abroad. A Companion to the "Pickwick Papers," by "Boz." One vol. Price 75 cents.

Queen Joanna; or, the Mysteries of the Court of Naples. Price 75 cents.

Mary Stuart, Queen of Scots. Complete in one large 8vo. vol. Price 75 cents.

May Middleton ; or, The History of a Fortune. Price 75 cents.

The Loves of the Harem. Price 50 cents.

The Discarded Queen. One volume. 50 cents.

Ellen Percy ; or, Memoirs of an Actress. 75 cents.

Massacre of Glencoe. Price 75 cents.

Agnes Evelyn ; or, Beauty and Pleasure. 75 cts.

The Parricide. Beautifully Illustrated. 75 cts.

Life in Paris. Handsomely Illustrated. 50 cts.

The Soldier's Wife. Illustrated. 75 cents.

Clifford and the Actress. Price 50 cents.

Edgar Montrose. One volume. Price 50 cents.

J. A. MAITLAND'S GREAT WORKS.

The Three Cousins. By J. A. Maitland. One vol., paper. Price $1.50; or in one vol., cloth, $2.00.

The Watchman. Complete in one large vol., paper cover. Price $1.50; or in one vol., cloth, $2.00.

The Wanderer. Complete in one volume, paper cover. Price $1.50; or in one vol., cloth, for $2.00.

The Diary of an Old Doctor. One vol., paper cover. Price $1.50; or bound in cloth for $2.00.

The Lawyer's Story. One volume, paper cover. Price $1.50; or bound in cloth for $2.00.

Sartaroe. A Tale of Norway. One volume, paper cover. Price $1.50; or in cloth for $2.00.

CHARLES J. PETERSON'S WORKS.

The Old Stone Mansion. one volume, paper. Price $1.50; or in cloth, for $2.00.

Kate Aylesford. A Love Story. One vol., paper. Price $1.50; or in one volume, cloth, for $2.00.

Cruising in the Last War. Complete in one volume. Price 75 cents.

The Valley Farm ; or, The Autobiography of an Orphan. Price 25 cents.

Grace Dudley ; or, Arnold at Saratoga. 25 cents

Copies of any of the above Works will be sent, Free of Postage, on Receipt of Retail Price,
By T. B. PETERSON & BROTHERS, Philadelphia, Pa.

10   T. B. PETERSON & BROTHERS' LIST OF PUBLICATIONS.

WAVERLEY NOVELS.

The Waverley Novels. By Sir Walter Scott. With a magnificent Portrait of Sir Walter Scott, engraved from the last Portrait for which he ever sat, at Abbotsford, with his Autograph under it. This edition is complete in Five large octavo volumes, with handsomely engraved steel Title 'Pages to each volume, the whole being neatly and handsomely bound in cloth. This is the cheapest and most complete and perfect edition of the Waverley Novels published in the world, as it contains all the Author's last additions and corrections. Price Twelve Dollars for a complete and entire set bound in 5 vols., cloth.

CHEAP EDITION IN PAPER COVER.

This edition is published in Twenty-Six volumes, paper cover, price Fifty cents each, or the whole twenty-six volumes will be sold or sent to any one, free of postage, for Ten Dollars.

The following are their names.

The Heart of Mid Lothian,
Guy Mannering,
The Antiquary,
Old Mortality,
St. Ronan's Well,
Ivanhoe,
Rob Roy,
Waverley,
The Bride of Lammermoor,
Highland Widow,
Tales of a Grandfather,
Kenilworth,
Fair Maid of Perth,
Fortunes of Nigel,
Peveril of the Peak,
The Talisman, ·
Count Robert of Paris,
The Pirate,
The Abbot,
Red Gauntlet,
Quentin Durward,
The Monastery,
Woodstock,
Anne of Geierstein,
The Betrothed,
Castle Dangerous, and the Surgeon's Daughter,
Black Dwarf and Legend of Montrose.
Moredun. A Tale of 1210. Price 50 cents.
Lockhart's Life of Scott. Complete in one volume, cloth. With Portrait. Price $2.50.

WALTER SCOTT'S PROSE AND POETICAL WORKS.

We also publish Sir Walter Scott's complete Prose and Poetical Works, in ten large octavo volumes, bound in cloth. This edition contains every thing ever written by Sir Walter Scott. Price Twenty-four Dollars for a complete set.

GREEN'S WORKS ON GAMBLING.

Gambling Exposed. By J. H. Green, the Reformed Gambler. One vol., paper cover. Price $1.50; or in one volume, cloth, gilt, for $2.00.
The Secret Band of Brothers. One volume, paper cover. Price $1.50; or bound in one volume, cloth, for $2.00.
The Gambler's Life. One vol., paper cover. Price $1.50; or in one vol., cloth, gilt, for $2.00.
The Reformed Gambler. One vol., paper. Price $1.50; or in one vol., cloth, for $1.50.

HUMOROUS AMERICAN WORKS.

Original Illustrations by Darley and Others.

Done up in Illuminated Covers.

Being the most Humorous and Laughable Books ever printed in the English Language.

Major Jones' Courtship. With Thirteen Illustrations, from designs by Darley. Price 75 cents.
Drama in Pokerville. By J. M. Field. With Illustrations by Darley. Price 75 cents. .
Louisiana Swamp Doctor. By author of "Cupping on the Sternum." Illustrated by Darley. Price 75 cents.
Charcoal Sketches. By Joseph C. Neal. With Illustrations. Price 75 cents.
Yankee Amongst the Mermaids. By W. E. Burton. With Illustrations by Darley. 75 cents
Misfortunes of Peter Faber. By Joseph C. Neal. With Illustrations by Darley. Price 75 cents.
Major Jones' Sketches of Travel. With Illustrations, from designs by Darley. Price 75 cents.
Quarter Race in Kentucky. By W. T. Porter, Esq. With Illustrations by Darley. 75 cents
Sol. Smith's Theatrical Apprenticeship. Illustrated by Darley. Price 75 cents.
Yankee Yarns and Yankee Letters. By Sam Slick, alias Judge Haliburton. Price 75 cents.
Big Bear of Arkansas. Edited by Wm. T. Porter. With Illustrations by Darley. Price 75 cents.
Major Jones' Chronicles of Pineville. With Illustrations by Darley. Price 75 cents.
Life and Adventures of Percival Maberry. By J. H. Ingraham. Price 75 cents.
Frank Forester's Quorndon Hounds. By H. W. Herbert. With Illustrations. Price 75 cts.
Pickings from the "Picayune." With Illustrations by Darley. Price 75 cents.
Frank Forester's Shooting Box. With Illustrations by Darley. Price 75 cents.
Peter Ploddy. By author of "Charcoal Sketches." With Illustrations by Darley. Price 75 cents.
Western Scenes; or, Life on the Prairie. Illustrated by Darley. Price 75 cents. .
Streaks of Squatter Life. By author of "Major Jones' Courtship." Illustrated by Darley. Price 75 cents.
Simon Suggs.—Adventures of Captain Simon Suggs. Illustrated by Darley. 75 cents.
Stray Subjects Arrested and Bound Over. With Illustrations by Darley. 75 cents
Frank Forester's Deer Stalkers. With Illustrations. Price 75 cents.
Adventures of Captain Farrago. By Hon. H. H. Brackenridge. Illustrated. Price 75 cents.
Widow Rugby's Husband. By author of "Simon Suggs." With Illustrations. Price 75 cents.
Major O'Regan's Adventures. By Hon. H. H. Brackenridge. With Illustrations by Darley. Price 75 cents. · .
Theatrical Journey-Work and Anecdotal Recollections of Sol. Smith, Esq. Price 75 cents.
Polly Peablossom's Wedding. By the author of "Major Jones' Courtship." Price 75 cents.
Frank Forester's Warwick Woodlands. With beautiful Illustrations. Price 75 cents.
New Orleans Sketch Book. By "Stahl." With Illustrations by Darley. Price 75 cents.
The Love Scrapes of Fudge Fumble. By author of "Arkansaw Doctor." Price 75 cents.
The Mysteries of the Backwood. By "Tom Owen, the Bee Hunter." Price 75 cents.
Aunt Patty's Scrap Bag. By Mrs. Caroline Lee Hentz. Price 75 cents.
American Joe Miller. With 100 Illustrations. Price 50 cents.
Judge Haliburton's Yankee Stories. One vol., paper cover. Price $1.50; or cloth, $2.00.

Copies of any of the above Works will be sent, Free of Postage, on Receipt of Retail Price, By T. B. PETERSON & BROTHERS, Philadelphia, Pa.

GUSTAVE AIMARD'S WORKS.

The Prairie Flower. Price 75 cents.
The Indian Scout. Price 75 cents.
The Trail Hunter. Price 75 cents.
The Indian Chief. Price 75 cents.
The Red Track. Price 75 cents.
The Pirates of the Prairies. Price 75 cents.
The Trapper's Daughter. Price 75 cents.
The Tiger Slayer. Price 75 cents.
The Gold Seekers. Price 75 cents.
The Smuggler Chief. Price 75 cents.

All of Aimard's other books are in press by us.

LADIES' GUIDE TO POLITENESS.

The Ladies' Guide to True Politeness and Perfect Manners. By Miss Leslie. Cloth, full gilt back. Price $2.00.
The Ladies' Complete Guide to Needlework and Embroidery. 113 Illustrations. Cloth, gilt back. Price $2.00.
Ladies' Work Table Book. With Illustrations and full gilt back, cloth. Price $1.50.

GEORGE SAND'S WORKS.

Consuelo. By George Sand. Translated from the French, by Fayette Robinson. Complete and unabridged. One volume. Price 75 cents.
Countess of Rudolstadt. The Sequel to "Consuelo." Translated from the original French. Complete and unabridged edition. Price 75 cents.
Consuelo and Countess of Rudolstadt. Fine edition, both in one vol., cloth, $2.00.
Indiana. By author of "Consuelo," etc. A very bewitching and interesting work. One volume, paper cover. $1.50; or in one vol., cloth, for $2.00.
First and True Love. By author of "Consuelo," "Indiana," etc. Illustrated. Price 75 cents.
The Corsair. A Venetian Tale. One volume. Price 50 cents.

HUMOROUS ILLUSTRATED WORKS.

Neal's Charcoal Sketches. Three books in one volume, cloth, with 21 Illustrations, from original designs, by Felix O. C. Darley. Price $2.50.
High Life in New York. By Jonathan Slick. Beautifully Illustrated. One vol., paper cover, $1.50; or bound in one vol., cloth, $2.00.
Sam Slick, the Clockmaker. By Judge Haliburton. Illustrated. One volume, cloth, $2.00; or in one volume, paper cover, for $1.50.
Major Jones' Courtship and Travels. Beautifully illustrated. Complete in one volume, bound in cloth. Price $2.00.
Major Jones' Scenes in Georgia. Full of beautiful Illustrations. Complete in one volume, bound in cloth. Price $2.00.
Simon Suggs' Adventures and Travels. Illustrated. Complete in one volume, bound in cloth. Price $2.00.
Major Thorpe's Scenes in Arkansaw: With Sixteen illustrations from Designs by Darley. Complete in one vol., cloth. Price $2.00.
Modern Chivalry. By H. H. Brackenridge. One volume, cloth, gilt back. Price $2.00.
Humors of Falconbridge. One vol., paper cover. Price $1.50, or in one vol., cloth, for $2.00.
Piney Woods Tavern; or, Sam Slick in Texas. Cloth, $2.00; or in 1 vol., paper cover, $1.50.
Yankee Stories. By Judge Haliburton. One vol., paper cover. Price $1.50; or bound in cloth, for $2.00.
The Swamp Doctor's Adventures in the South-West. With 14 Illustrations from designs by Darley. Cloth. Price $2.00.
The Big Bear's Adventures and Travels: With Eighteen Illustrations from Original Designs by Darley. One vol., bound. Price $2.00.
Frank Forester's Sporting Scenes and Characters. Illustrated. Two vols., cloth, $4.00.

MISS BREMER'S NEW WORKS.

The Father and Daughter. By Fredrika Bremer. One vol. paper. Price $1.50; or cloth $2.00.
The Four Sisters. One vol., paper cover. Price $1.50; or in one volume cloth, for $2.00.
The Neighbors. One vol., paper cover. Price $1.50; or in one volume cloth, for $2.00.
The Home. One volume, paper cover. Price $1.50; or in one volume, cloth, for $2.00.
Life in the Old World; or, Two Years in Switzerland and Italy. Complete in two large duodecimo volumes, of near 1000 pages. Price $4.00.

GEORGE LIPPARD'S WORKS.

The Empire City; or, New York by Night and Day; its Aristocracy and its Dollars. Price 75 cts.
Memoirs of a Preacher; or, the Mysteries of the Pulpit. Full of illustrations. Price 75 cents.
Washington and his Men; or, the Second Series of the Legends of the Revolution. Price 75 cts.
The Mysteries of Florence. Complete in one large octavo volume. Price $1.00.
Legends of the American Revolution; or, Washington and his Generals. Price $1.50.
The Quaker City; or, The Monks of Monk Hall. Complete in one large octavo volume. Price $1.50.
Paul Ardenheim; the Monk of Wissahickon. Complete in one large octavo volume. Price $1.50
Blanche of Brandywine. A Romance of the American Revolution. Price $1.50.
The Entranced; or, the Wanderer of Eighteen Centuries. Price 25 cents.
The Nazarene. Price 75 cents.
Legends of Mexico. Price 50 cents.
The Bank Director's Son. Price 25 cents.
The Ride with the Dead. Price 50 cents.
The Robbers. By Frederick Schiller. With a Preface, by George Lippard. Price 25 cents.

DOW'S PATENT SERMONS.

☞ Each volume, or series, is complete in itself, and volumes are sold separately to any one, or in sets.

Dow's Short Patent Sermons. First Series. By Dow, Jr. Containing 128 Sermons. Complete in one vol., bound in cloth, for $1.50; or in one vol., paper, for $1.00.
Dow's Short Patent Sermons. Second Series. By Dow, Jr. Containing 144 Sermons. Complete in one vol., bound in cloth, for $1.50; or in one vol., paper, for $1.00.
Dow's Short Patent Sermons. Third Series. By Dow, Jr. Containing 116 Sermons. Complete in one vol., bound in cloth, for $1.50; or in one vol., paper, for $1.00.
Dow's Short Patent Sermons. Fourth Series. By Dow, Jr. Containing 152 Sermons. Complete in one vol., bound in cloth, for $1.50; or in one vol., paper, for $1.00.

EUGENE SUE'S GREAT NOVELS.

Illustrated Wandering Jew. With Eighty-seven large Illustrations. Complete in one large octavo volume, paper cover. Price $1.50; or in one volume, cloth, for $2.00.
Mysteries of Paris; and Gerolstein, the Sequel to it. Complete in one vol., paper cover. Price $1.50; or in one vol., cloth, for $2.00.
Martin the Foundling. Illustrated. Paper cover. Price $1.50; or in cloth, $2.00.
First Love. Price 50 cents.
Woman's Love. Illustrated. Price 50 cents.
The Man-of-War's-Man. Price 25 cents.
The Female Bluebeard. Price 50 cents.
Raoul De Surville. Price 25 cents.

SIR E. L. BULWER'S NOVELS.

The Roue; or, The Hazards of Women. 50 cents.
The Oxonians. A Sequel to "The Roue." 50 cts.
Falkland. A Novel. One vol., octavo. 25 cents.
The Courtier. By Sir E. L. Bulwer. 25 cents.

PETERSONS' "ILLUMINATED" STORIES.
PRICE 25 CENTS EACH.
Each Book in an Illuminated Cover, in five colors, and full of Illustrations.

The Flying Artillerist,.......... *Price* 25	Morgan, the Buccaneer,........ *Price* 25
The Rebel Bride,....................... 25	Lives of the Felons,................... 25
Old Put; or, Days of '76,............ 25	Joseph T. Hare,..................... 25
The King's Cruisers,................. 25	Kit Clayton,........................... 25
The Flying Yankee,............ 25	Alexander Tardy,................... 25
Gallant Tom,............................ 25	Seven Brothers of Wyoming,.... 25
The Doomed Ship,.................... 25	Silver and Pewter,................ 25
Jack Junk,.............................. 25	Ninon de L'Enclos,............... 25
Harry Helm, ... 25	The River Pirates,................. 25
Harry Tempest,....................... 25	Dark Shades of City Life,......... 25
Rebel and the Rover,............... 25	Female Life in New York,....... 25
The Yankee Middy,.................. 25	Rats of the Seine,.................. 25
Galloping Gus,........................ 25	Mysteries of Bedlam,.............. 25
Sylvia Seabury,....................... 25	Charles Ransford,................ 25
Sweeny Todd,.......................... 25	Eveleen Wilson,.................... 25
The Gold Seekers,................... 25	The Iron Cross,..................... 25
Valdez, the Pirate,.................. 25	Biddy Woodhull,.................... 25
Nat Blake,............................. 25	Mysteries of a Convent,......... 25
Tom Waters,............................ 25	Man-of-War's-Man,................ 25
Ned Hastings,......................... 25	The Mysterious Marriage,....... 25
Bill Horton,............................ 25	Captain Blood, the Highwayman, 25
Dick Parker,........................... 25	Captain Blood and the Beagles,... 25
Jack Ketch,............................ 25	The Highwayman's Avenger,...... 25
Mother Brownrigg,.................. 25	Rody the Rover,..................... 25
Galloping Dick,....................... 25	16-Stringed-Jack's Fight for Life,. 25
Mary Bateman,....................... 25	Jonathan Wild,..................... 25
Raoul de Surville,.................... 25	Rose Warrington,.................. 25
The Robber's Wife,.................. 25	Ghost Stories,........................ 25
Obi; or, Three-Fingered Jack,... 25	Arthur Spring,...................... 25
Desperadoes New World,.......... 25	Davis, the Pirate,................. 25
Harry Thomas,........................ 25	The Pirate's Son,.................. 25
Mrs. Whipple and Jesse Strang,... 25	The Valley Farm,.................. 25

☞ The above List of Books will be found to be the most saleable ever printed in this coun
try. Booksellers will be supplied with them by the hundred or thousand at very low rates.

PETERSONS' DETECTOR AND BANK NOTE LIST.

Monthly, per annum,.................$1.50	Single Numbers,..........................15 cents
Semi-Monthly, per annum,............ 3.00	To Agents, a hundred, net cash......$10.00

Subscriptions may commence with any number. Terms cash in advance. There is no better ad-
vertising medium to reach the business community throughout the country than PETERSONS' DE-
TECTOR. Its circulation among the enterprising storekeepers, mechanics, farmers, merchants and
manufacturers is very large and increasing. Advertisements inserted in PETERSONS' DETECTOR
will be seen by a large portion of the active and energetic people of the United States, and our
terms are lower than any other journal with the same circulation and influence.

CHEAPEST BOOK HOUSE IN THE WORLD.
To Libraries! Booksellers! News Agents! Pedlers! Etc.

Any person wanting books had better send on their orders at once to the "CHEAP BOOKSEL-
LING AND PUBLISHING HOUSE OF T. B. PETERSON & BROTHERS, No. 306 Chestnut
Street, Philadelphia, who have the largest stock in the country, and will supply them at very low
rates. We have just issued a new and complete Catalogue, as well as wholesale price Lists, which
we send to Booksellers and Libraries on application.

Enclose five, ten, twenty, fifty or a hundred dollars, or more, to us in a letter, and write
what kind of books you wish, and they will be packed and sent to you at once, per first express or
mail, or any way you may direct, with circulars, show bills, etc., gratis. All we ask is to give us a trial.

Orders solicited from Libraries, Booksellers, Canvassers, News Agents, and all others in want of
good and fast selling books, and they will please send on their orders.

Agents and Canvassers are requested to send for our Canvassers' Confidential Circular containing
instructions. Address all cash orders, retail or wholesale, to

T. B. PETERSON & BROTHERS, 306 Chestnut St., Philadelphia, Pa.

T. B. PETERSON & BROTHERS' PUBLICATIONS.

The Books on this page will be found to be the very Best and Latest Publications in the world, and are Published and for Sale by T. B. PETERSON & BROTHERS, Philadelphia.

CAPT. MARRYATT'S WORKS.

Jacob Faithful,	50	Newton Foster, -	50
Japhet Search of Father,	50	King's Own, -	50
Phantom Ship, -	50	Pirate & Three Cutters,	50
Midshipman Easy, -	50	Peter Simple, -	50
Pacha of Many Tales,	50	Percival Keene, -	50
Naval Officer, - -	50	Poor Jack, - -	50
Snarleyow, - -	50	Sea King, - -	50

LIVES OF HIGHWAYMEN.

Life of John A. Murrel,	50	Biddy Woodhull, -	25
Life of Joseph T. Hare,	25	Eveleen Wilson, -	25
Life of Monroe Edwards,	50	Diary of a Pawnbroker,	50
Life of Helen Jewett,	50	Silver and Pewter, -	25
Life of Jack Rann, -	50	Sweeney Todd, - -	25
Life of Jonathan Wild,	25	Life of Mother Brownrig,	25
Life of Henry Thomas,	25	Dick Parker, the Pirate,	25
Life of Dick Turpin,	50	Life of Mary Bateman,	25
Life of Arthur Spring,	25	Life of Captain Blood,	25
Life of Jack Ketch, -	25	Life of Galloping Dick,	25
Ninon De L'Enclos, -	25	Sixteen-Stringed Jack's	
Desperadoes New World,	25	Fight for Life, -	25
Mysteries of N. Orleans,	50	Highwayman's Avenger,	25
The Robber's Wife, -	25	Life of Raoul De Surville	25
Obi, or 3 Fingered Jack,	25	Life of Sybil Grey, -	50
Kit Clayton, - -	25	Life of Rody the Rover,	25
Lives of the Felons, -	25	Captain Blood and the	
Tom Waters, - -	25	Beagles, - -	25
Life of Mrs. Whipple &		Life of Grace O'Malley,	50
Jesse Straag, -	25	Life of Jack Sheppard,	50
Nat Blake, - -	25	Life of Davy Crockett,	25
Bill Horton, - -	25	Life of Guy Fawkes,	75
Galloping Gus, - -	25	Life and Adventures	
Ned Hastings, - -	25	of Vidocq, - -	1 50

SEA TALES.

Adventures Ben Brace,	75	Yankees in Japan, -	25
Jack Adams, Mutineer,	75	Charles Ransford, -	25
Jack Ariel's Adventures,	75	Morgan, the Buccaneer,	25
Petrel, or Life on Ocean,	50	Jack Junk, - -	25
Cruising in Last War,	50	Davis, the Pirate, -	25
Life of Paul Periwinkle,	75	Valdez, the Pirate,	25
Percy Effingham, -	75	The Iron Cross, -	25
Life of Tom Bowling,	75	Gallant Tom, -	25
The Three Pirates, -	50	Harry Helm, - -	25
The Flying Dutchman,	50	Harry Tempest, -	25
Red King, - -	50	Rebel and Rover, -	25
The Corsair, - -	50	Jacob Faithful, -	50
Yankee Jack, - -	50	Phantom Ship, -	50
Red Wing, - -	50	Midshipman Easy, -	50
The Pirate's Son, -	25	Pacha of Many Tales,	50
The Doomed Ship, -	25	Naval Officer, -	50
Life of Alexander Tardy,	25	Snarleyow, - -	50
The Flying Yankee, -	25	Newton Foster, -	50
The Yankee Middy, -	25	King's Own, -	50
The Gold Seekers, -	25	Japhet, - -	50
The River Pirates, -	25	Pirate & Three Cutters	50
The King's Cruisers, -	25	Peter Simple, -	50
Man-of-Wars-Man, -	25	Percival Keene, -	50
Dark Shades City Life,	25	Poor Jack, - -	50
The Rats of the Seine,	25	Sea King, - -	50

AINSWORTH'S GREAT WORKS.

Life of Jack Sheppard,	50	Dick Turpin, -	50
Life of Davy Crockett,	50	Life of Henry Thomas,	25
Guy Fawkes, - -	75	Life of Mrs. Whipple	25
The Star Chamber, -	75	Desperadoes New World,	25
Old St. Paul's, - -	75	Ninon De L'Enclos, -	25
Mysteries of the Court		Life of Arthur Spring,	25
of Queen Anne, -	75	Life of Grace O'Malley,	50
Mysteries Court Stuarts,	75	Tower of London, 2 vls.	1 00
Windsor Castle, - -	75	Miser's Daughter, do.	1 00

GEORGE SAND'S WORKS.

Consuelo, - -	75	The Corsair, -	50
Countess of Rudolstadt,	75	Indiana, 1 vol., paper,	1 50
First and True Love,	75	or in 1 vol., cloth	2 00
Consuelo and Countess of Rudolstadt, 1 vol , cloth, $2.00			

HARRY COCKTON'S WORKS.

Sylvester Sound, -	75	The Sisters, - -	75
Valentine Vox, the		The Steward, -	75
Ventriloquist, -	75	Percy Effngham, -	75

MILITARY AND ARMY BOOKS.

Ellsworth's Zouave Drill,	25	The Soldier's Companion,	25
U. S. Light Infantry Drill,	25	Volunteer's Text Book,	50
U. S. Government Infan-		The Soldier's Guide,	25
try & Rifle Tactics, -	25		

SMITH'S WORKS.

The Usurer's Victim; or		Adelaide Waldgrave, or	
Thomas Balscombe,	50	Trials of a Governess,	50

CHRISTY & WHITE'S SONG BOOKS.

Christy and Wood's		Serenader's Song Book,	13
Complete Song Book,	13	Budworth's Songs, -	13
Melodeon Song Book,	13	Christy and White's	
Plantation Melodies,	13	Complete Ethiopian	
Ethiopian Song Book,	13	Melodies. Cloth, -	1 00

EUGENE SUE'S WORKS.

Wandering Jew, -	1 50	Female Bluebeard, -	1 50
Mysteries of Paris, -	1 50	Man-of-War's-Man, -	25
Martin, the Foundling,	1 50	Life and Adventures	
First Love, - -	50	of Raoul De Surville,	25
Woman's Love, -	50		

DR. HOLLICK'S WORKS.

Dr. Hollick's great work on Anatomy and Phys-		
iology of the Human Figure, with plates, -	-	1 50
Dr. Hollick's Family Physician, - - -	-	25

REVOLUTIONARY TALES.

Seven Bros. of Wyoming,	25	Wau-nan-gee, -	50
The Brigand, - -	50	Legends of Mexico,	50
The Rebel Bride, -	25	Grace Dudley; or Ar-	
Ralph Runnlon, -	50	nold at Saratoga, -	25
The Flying Artillerist,	25	The Guerilla Chief,	75
Old Put, - -	25	The Quaker Soldier, -	1 50

EMERSON BENNETT'S WORKS.

The Border Rover, -	1 50	Bride of Wilderness,	1 50
Clara Moreland, -	1 50	Ellen Norbury, -	50
Viola; or Adventures		Forged W.ll, -	1 50
in Far South-West,	1 50	Kate Clarendon, -	1 50

Above are each in paper cover, or in cloth, $2.00.

Heiress of Bellefonte,		Pioneer's Daughter and	
and Walde-Warren,	50	Unknown Countess,	50

T. S. ARTHUR'S WORKS.

The Two Brides, -	25	The Divorced Wife, -	25
Love in a Cottage,	25	Pride and Prudence, -	25
Love in High Life, -	25	Agnes, or the Possessed,	25
Year after Marriage, -	25	Lucy Sandford, -	25
The Lady at Home, -	25	The Banker's Wife, -	25
Cecelia Howard, -	25	The Two Merchants, -	25
Orphan Children, -	50	Insubordination, -	50
Debtor's Daughter, -	25	The Iron Rule, -	25
Mary Moreton, -	25	Lizzie Glenn; or the	
Trial and Triumph, -	25	Trials of a Seamstress	1 50
Six Nights with the Washingtonians. Illustrated,			1 50

MRS. GREY'S WORKS.

Cousin Harry, -	1 50	The Little Beauty, -	1 50

The above are each in one volume, paper cover. Each book is also in one volume, cloth, price $2.00 each.

Gipsey's Daughter, -	50	Old Dower House, -	50
Lena Cameron, -	50	Hyacinthe, - -	50
Belle of the Family, -	50	Alice Seymour, -	25
Sybil Lennard, -	50	Mary Seaham, -	75
Duke and Cousin, -	50	Passion and Principle,	75
The Little Wife, -	50	The Flirt, - -	75
Manœuvring Mother,	50	Good Society, -	75
Baronet's Daughter's,	50	Lion Hearted, -	75
Young Prima Donna,	50		

SIR WALTER SCOTT'S NOVELS.

Ivanhoe, - -	50	St. Ronan's Well, -	50
Rob Roy, - -	50	Red Gauntlet, -	50
Guy Mannering, -	50	The Betrothed, -	50
The Antiquary, -	50	The Talisman, -	50
Old Mortality, -	50	Woodstock, - -	50
Heart of Mid Lothian,	50	Highland Widow, etc.,	50
Bride of Lammermoor,	50	The Fair Maid of Perth,	50
Waverly, - -	50	Anne of Geierstein, -	50
Kenilworth, - -	50	Count Robert of Paris,	50
The Pirate, - -	50	The Black Dwarf and	
The Monastery, -	50	Legend of Montrose,	50
The Abbot, - -	50	Castle Dangerous, and	
The Fortunes of Nigel,	50	Surgeon's Daughter,	50
Peveril of the Peak, -	50	Moredun. A Tale of	
Quentin Durward, -	50	1210, - -	50
Tales of a Grandfather,	50	Life of Scott, cloth, -	2 00

A complete set of the novels of Walter Scott will be sent to any one, to any place, free of postage, for Ten Dollars; or another edition of Waverly Novels, in five volumes, in cloth, for $12.00; or the Complete Prose and Poetical Works of Sir Walter Scott, in ten vols, cloth, for $24.00.

GEORGE LIPPARD'S WORKS.

The Empire City, -	75	The Entranced, -	25
Memoirs of a Preacher,	75	Washington and his	
The Quaker City, -	1 50	Generals, or Legends	
Paul Ardenheim, -	1 50	of the Revolution,	1 50
Blanche Brandywine,	1 50	Ride with the Dead,	50
Mysteries of Florence,	1 00	Legends of Mexico,	50
The Nazarene, -	75	Bank Director's Son,	25
Washington and his Men	75	The Robbers, -	25

LIEBIG'S WORKS ON CHEMISTRY.

Agricultural Chemistry,	25	Liebig's celebrated Let-	
Animal Chemistry, -	25	ters on Potato Disease,	25
Liebig's Complete Works on Chemistry. Containing everything written by Professor Liebig, is also issued in one large volume, bound in cloth. Price $2.00.			

E. L. BULWER'S NOVELS.

		Falkland, - -	25
The Roue, - -	50		
The Oxonian, - -	50	The Courtier, -	25

☞ Copies of any of the above Works will be sent by Mail, free of Postage, to any part of the United States, on receipt of the retail price, by T. B. Peterson & Brothers, Philadelphia.

www.ingramcontent.com/pod-product-compliance
Lightning Source LLC
Chambersburg PA
CBHW022041080426
42733CB00007B/936